Armies of Arthurian Britain

Gabriele Esposito is a military historian who works as a freelance author and researcher for some of the most important publishing houses in the military history sector. In particular, he is an expert specializing in uniformology: his interests and expertise range from the ancient civilizations to modern post-colonial conflicts. During recent years, he has conducted and published several researches on the military history of the Latin American countries, with special attention on the War of the Triple Alliance and the War of the Pacific. He is among the leading experts on the military history of the Italian Wars of Unification and the Spanish Carlist Wars. His books and essays are published on a regular basis by Osprey Publishing, Winged Hussar Publishing and Libreria Editrice Goriziana; he is also the author of numerous military history articles appearing in specialized magazines such as *Ancient Warfare Magazine*, *Medieval Warfare Magazine*, *The Armourer*, *History of War*, *Guerres et Histoire*, *Focus Storia* and *Focus Storia Wars*.

Armies of Arthurian Britain

History, Organization and Equipment

Gabriele Esposito

Pen & Sword
MILITARY

First published in Great Britain in 2026 by
Pen & Sword Military
An imprint of
Pen & Sword Books Limited
Yorkshire – Philadelphia

ISBN 978 1 03613 734 2

A CIP catalogue record for this book is
available from the British Library.

Typeset by Mac Style
Printed and bound in India by Replika Press Pvt. Ltd.

MIX
Paper | Supporting responsible forestry
FSC
www.fsc.org
FSC™ C016779

The Publisher's authorised representative in the EU for product
safety is Authorised Rep Compliance Ltd., Ground Floor,
71 Lower Baggot Street, Dublin D02 P593, Ireland.
www.arccompliance.com

For a complete list of Pen & Sword titles please contact

PEN & SWORD BOOKS LIMITED
47 Church Street, Barnsley, South Yorkshire, S70 2AS, England
E-mail: enquiries@pen-and-sword.co.uk
Website: www.pen-and-sword.co.uk
or
PEN AND SWORD BOOKS
1950 Lawrence Road, Havertown, PA 19083, USA
E-mail: uspen-and-sword@casematepublishers.com
Website: www.penandswordbooks.com

Contents

Acknowledgements

This book is dedicated to my magnificent parents, Maria Rosaria and Benedetto, for the immense love and fundamental support that they always give me. Thanks to their precious advice over many years, this book has turned out even better than I had planned. A very special thanks goes to Philip Sidnell, the commissioning editor of my books for Pen & Sword: his love for history and his passion for publishing are the key factors behind the success of our publications. Many thanks also to the production manager of this title, Matt Jones, for his excellent work and great enthusiasm. A special thanks is due to Tony Walton for editing my original manuscript with a keen eye and his usual breadth of knowledge. A very special mention goes to the brilliant reenactment groups that collaborated with their photographs to the creation of this book: without the incredible work of research of their members, the final result of this publication would not have been the same. As a result, I want to express my deep gratitude to the following living history associations: Protectores Domini Nostri from Italy, Letavia from France, Wulfheodenas from the United Kingdom and Uttaharjar from Scandinavia (Denmark, Norway and Sweden).

Introduction

Following the evacuation of Roman troops in AD 410, Britain entered a new phase of its history, one that was characterized by the co-existence of competing armed groups on British soil. The Britons, who had been progressively 'romanized' during the previous centuries, retained many elements of the military organization that was typical of the Late Empire, but these were mixed with other important components that came from pre-Roman Celtic traditions. In Wales, the romanization of the local population had never been fully carried out, as a result of which the Britons living in Welsh lands fought in a way that had evolved little from the pre-Roman era. The military forces of Sub-Roman Britain faced two main kinds of enemies from the early fifth century AD: Celtic peoples from Scotland or Ireland and Germanic communities from continental Europe. The Picts of Scotland and the Scots of Ireland were perceived as wild savages by most of the Britons, having never been submitted by Rome and thus preserving their 'primitive' Celtic nature. This was reflected in the kind of warfare that was practiced in Early Medieval Scotland and Ireland. The Saxons, Angles and Jutes who invaded Britain from the mid-fifth century had their own distinct Germanic military traditions, which they imported to the British Isles at the point of their swords. This book will detail the campaigns that took place in Britain from the central decades of the fourth century, ending its analysis with the final phase of the Saxon conquest. It will look at how the Late Roman system of military defence crumbled in Britannia and how its remnants gave birth to the Sub-Roman armies of what became known as the Arthurian Age. We will consider the most up-to-date scientific theories regarding the historical figure of Arthur and provide full details on the military history of the Britons' enemies: Picts, Scots, Saxons, Angles and Jutes. Finally, the book will include two chapters devoted to analysis of the organization and equipment of the various forces that fought in the campaigns in Britain between the mid-fourth and mid-seventh centuries.

Chapter 1

The Decadence of the Roman Empire

For centuries, the province of Britannia was one of the most flourishing territories of the Roman Empire, especially from an economic point of view. Britain, however, had a series of peculiarities compared with other areas of the Empire. First of all, it was not inhabited by a large number of Italic settlers due to its relative geographical isolation; secondly, its territory could be reached only by crossing the English Channel, with no land route. During the early decades of their presence in Britain, the Romans, under their famed general Agricola, had occupied most of present-day Scotland, but their presence there was extremely short-lived. Indeed, the Roman fortifications in the region that they called Caledonia were soon abandoned. Consequently, by the beginning of the Late Empire, the regions of the British Isles were characterized by a widely varied political situation. England was a rich Roman province, where the local Celtic culture had already been influenced by Rome, while Wales was Roman territory but retained a very strong Celtic identity as Roman cultural penetration had been slower and weaker in Welsh lands. Scotland was fully independent from the Romans, but had strong links with Britannia, and Ireland had little direct contact with the Romans but was fully integrated into the economic and political networks of the British Isles. After abandoning Scotland, the Romans built two massive, fortified lines to defend their British territories from incursions by the warlike Celtic communities of Caledonia: the southern Hadrian's Wall and the northern Antonine Wall. Nonetheless, Rome retained its original ambition of conquering Scotland, continuing to conduct military campaigns in Caledonia. These could be brief punitive expeditions organized to pacify the northern frontier of its British dominions or larger campaigns aimed at re-establishing a strong Roman presence in the Lowlands of Scotland.

By AD 200, however, the whole Roman Empire was no longer in an expansionist phase, the borders of its territories being fortified in order to protect Roman lands from external attacks. A long and heavily fortified *limes* (border) was created along the Rhine between Gaul and Germania, while another was established along the Danube in order to protect the Roman dominions extending from Noricum to Dacia (from modern Austria to Romania). In Britannia, the *limes* corresponded to Hadrian's Wall, which progressively acquired a more important defensive function.

Until AD 200, the Romans were strong enough to play an active role in the defence of their borders, anticipating the attacks of their enemies and conducting demonstrative raids to terrorize the communities living on the frontiers. With the beginning of the Crisis of the Third Century, however, the frontier policy changed dramatically, the Empire starting to experience great difficulties. Conventionally, the assassination of Emperor Severus Alexander in AD 235 is considered the starting point of the Crisis of the Third Century, but it should be noted that the Empire's internal and external troubles had started long before then. The first signs of military difficulties had become apparent during the reign of Marcus Aurelius, when the terrible Marcomannic Wars of AD 166–180 had revealed that the Germanic tribes of Northern and Central Europe were transforming themselves into a serious menace for Rome. Under severe pressure from warlike peoples migrating from the steppes of Central Asia, the Germani moved towards the borders of the Empire and started to be organized into large confederation of tribes that posed a strong military threat. The Empire was no longer ready to face an external invasion with its usual cohesion and internal stability. Indeed, the assassination of Severus Alexander led to the beginning of a series of civil wars that ravaged most Roman territory.

After several decades of internal prosperity and military expansionism on the borders, following the death of Marcus Aurelius in AD 180, the Roman Empire started to experience a general crisis that affected all its structures, including its military. This turbulent period of Roman history, commonly known as Crisis of the Third Century, lasted from AD 235 to the ascension of Diocletian in AD 284. Since the reign of Augustus, the Romans had abandoned their ambition to occupy Germany, but had been able to contain the Germanic peoples and to deal with their incursions. The *limes* – the border between the Roman Empire and the barbarians – had remained quiet and stable for a long time. The military supremacy of the Romans had never been contested, and relations with the Germani had generally remained quite positive. During the second half of the second century, however, this situation changed in a dramatic way. With warlike peoples migrating from the steppes of Central Asia and Eastern Europe, the Germani moved towards the borders of the Empire. For the first time in their recent history, the Romans had to face massive migrations of entire peoples, not just small raids by single tribes. The defensive system based on garrisons of legions and locally recruited auxiliaries could not handle the massive penetrations of the Germanic peoples now on the move. The border was too vast to be defended effectively, with simultaneous attacks from several different tribes becoming common. The confederation of Germanic tribes could assemble large numbers of warriors for attacks on particular sectors of the Roman *limes*. During the Marcomannic Wars, the Romans experienced further military difficulties, only being

Roman officer of the Late Empire wearing a muscle cuirass.
(*Photo by Rachele Lori, copyright by Protectores Domini Nostri*)

Roman officer of the Late Empire wearing a crested helmet of the ridge type. (*Photo by Rachele Lori, copyright by Protectores Domini Nostri*)

able to defeat the Germani after suffering severe battlefield losses. To this could be added the Antonine Plague, which killed thousands of people across the Empire, along with the constant state of war that existed on Rome's eastern borders, where the Parthians were militarily active. It was only thanks to the great leadership of Marcus Aurelius that the Roman Empire was able to survive the difficult period of the Marcomannic Wars, but many questions remained dangerously unresolved.

The immediate successors of Marcus Aurelius, from his son Commodus onwards, did very little to improve the Empire's defences. With the ascendancy of the new Severan Dynasty, the institutional nature of the Roman Empire was changed. Starting from Septimius Severus, the emperors began to be military despots, able to retain power only thanks to the support of the army and the equestrian social class. The traditional respect that the various emperors had shown towards the Senate started to disappear: the monarch had absolute power and could easily impose his will through the use of violence. The senatorial class gradually lost their importance, especially in the military, as loyalty towards the emperor became increasingly more important than virtue. As the soldiers were the real holders of power, emperors started to treat the army as their own private property. Large donatives of money were distributed to the legionaries, their pay was gradually augmented and the number of troops under direct control of the emperor was increased. Septimius Severus was the first monarch to garrison a legion near Rome. Furthermore, after winning the civil war that gave him the Empire, he replaced all the members of the Praetorian Guard with new men from his loyal legions stationed in Pannonia, who had showed their loyalty fighting on his side during the recent civil war. Another great political change, which happened in the eastern part of the Empire, had very important consequences for the military situation of the Romans. In AD 228, the Parthians, who had controlled present-day Iran since the fall of the Hellenistic Seleucid Empire, were decisively defeated by a new Persian dynasty that assumed control of their lands. The new rulers of Iran were the Sassanids, who soon decisively transformed the former Parthian Empire. The Parthians, hailing from the steppes of Central Asia, had created a feudal state that was a confederation of several different regions that had great autonomy. However, the Sassanids soon reorganized the Empire into a centralized nation with a strong ruler and a single religion.

As a result of all these changes, the eastern part of the Roman Empire started to be menaced by a new threat that was much more dangerous than the Parthians. The Sassanids had a political organization that was in many aspects very similar to that of the Romans, and thus could confront the Roman Empire on almost equal terms. While the Parthians had generally limited themselves to raids and guerrilla campaigns, the Sassanids were capable of launching full-scale invasions of the rich

Roman officer of the Late Empire wearing a *pileus pannonicus* cap made of fur. (*Photo by Rachele Lori, copyright by Protectores Domini Nostri*)

Roman senior officer from the Late Empire wearing a distinctive helmet adorned with peacock feathers. (*Photo by Rachele Lori, copyright by Protectores Domini Nostri*)

Roman eastern provinces. Since the ascendancy of the new dynasty, the state of war on the eastern *limes* was almost continuous. In AD 260, Emperor Valerian was defeated in battle and captured by the Sassanids, heralding one of the worst crises in the long history of Rome. With no more central authority to speak of, the Empire risked disappearing forever as a result of internal secessions and external invasions. Many thousands of Germanic warriors crossed the Roman borders and laid waste to large areas of the northern provinces, while the Sassanids found no opposition in their occupation of large parts of the eastern territories. At this point, to more effectively face the foreign invasions, two large parts of the Empire abandoned the central government and started to act as independent political entities. The territories of modern France, Britain and Spain proclaimed their independence as the Gallic Empire, while most of the eastern provinces were absorbed into the Kingdom of Palmyra. Until the rise of the Sassanids, the desert city of Palmyra had been a small client state of Rome, having great commercial importance but very limited political power. The defeat of Valerian, however, swiftly changed all this, with Odenatus, the king of Palmyra, taking the opportunity of this political vacuum to enlarge his territories. He presented himself as the legitimate defender of Roman interests in the East because of his alliance with Rome, and was able to unite most of the eastern provinces under his direct control and launch a strong counter-offensive against the Sassanids.

Judging the secessions of the third century from a historical point of view, it was only thanks to them that the Roman Empire was able to survive. The division of imperial lands enabled the local leaders and their military forces to put up a better defence against foreign invasions. This was the case in Gaul, where the usurper Postumus was able to defeat the Germani; more or less the same happened in Syria and Egypt, where Odenatus contained the Sassanid advances. The Gallic Empire remained an independent state during the period AD 260–274, while the Kingdom of Palmyra acted as a free country from AD 261 up to AD 272. Both secessions were definitively crushed by Emperor Aurelianus, who was also able to effectively fight Rome's external enemies. The entire period of the Crisis of the Third Century is also known as the Military Anarchy, because it saw total chaos in the successions of emperors caused by the increasing power of the military. From the reign of Septimius Severus, the Roman monarchs started to be chosen by the Praetorian Guard or the Roman Army: the dynastic principle, which had worked quite well until then, was completely abandoned after the assassination of Severus Alexander, who was killed by his own troops. The legions, which were now mostly commanded by officers from the *equites* social class, began to kill and proclaim emperors according to their own interests. It was enough to offer a large donative to the Praetorians or the legionaries

Roman heavy infantrymen from the Late Empire wearing scale armour.
(*Photo by Rachele Lori, copyright by Protectores Domini Nostri*)

to obtain the throne, while reducing the pay of soldiers would lead to an emperor being deposed or killed. The weakness of the senatorial class and the continuous state of military emergency gave all political power to the military leaders, a state of affairs that temporarily ended only with the ascendancy of Diocletian. The Crisis of the Third Century, however, was not only felt politically and militarily one. It also seriously reduced the demographic capabilities of the Empire due to the deaths

Roman officers from the Late Empire. The figure on the right is wearing the clothes that were used when off duty. (*Photo by Rachele Lori, copyright by Protectores Domini Nostri*)

caused by numerous terrible epidemics. Furthermore, the economy and commerce were severely damaged, while the traditional Roman way of life also had to change in a notable way. New religions gradually became dominant and Roman society completely changed its internal organization.

Traditionally, since the Late Republic, the Romans had developed a social structure that was based on three main classes: the aristocracy (senatorial families), *equites* (more or less a middle class) and the plebs (the lowest social group). The enormous difficulties of the Crisis reduced the number of social classes from three to two: the richest members of society – the aristocracy and the wealthiest *equites* – started to form a new group known as the *honestiores*; the modest *equites* and the plebs, meanwhile, started to be known as *humiliores*. In practice, the Crisis had cancelled the middle class: the inhabitants of the Empire were now either extremely rich or extremely poor. The most important *equites* had transformed themselves into a new ruling class, gradually making the traditional aristocracy of the senators more marginal. Obviously this had very serious effects on the leadership of the army, as we shall see. To all this can be added another important social change, which happened before the beginning of the Crisis. In AD 212, the Constitutio Antoniana of Emperor Caracalla gave Roman citizenship to all the inhabitants of the Empire. Until that moment, the Roman military organization had been based on the distinction between citizens and non-citizens. With the promulgation of the Constitutio Antoniana, the main social difference between legionaries and auxiliaries was completely cancelled. Differently from what happened previously, a provincial man now did not have to serve in the army as an auxiliary for years in order to obtain Roman citizenship. Finally, it is important to note how the Crisis had a deep impact over the urban centres of the Empire. Many historians have defined Roman civilization as an 'empire of the cities', because urban centres were the real core of the Roman state. The Crisis changed all this. The large, open and rich cities of previous decades were progressively abandoned due to the fear of foreign attacks; new smaller cities started to be built, which were protected by defensive walls and were thus much more isolated and poor than before. The city of Rome was encircled by new walls, construction of which began under Emperor Aurelian. From an economic point of view, the western provinces became increasingly poor due to them being exposed to foreign attacks; the eastern provinces, instead, became increasingly rich thanks to their superior agricultural capabilities. The economic decline of the western territories affected the monetary system, with a decreasing circulation of gold and silver coinage. This altered the commercial balance of the Roman Empire's market in a decisive way, progressively destroying the economic integration of Roman territories.

The long Crisis of the Third Century ended only with the ascension to power of Diocletian in AD 284. After decades of internal unrest, civil wars, secessions and foreign invasions, the Empire was in a traumatic situation. Although Roman civilization had survived and the Empire had retained territorial unity, all the institutions of the state were experiencing severe difficulties. Diocletian quickly understood that the political and military structures of the Empire had to be completely reformed in order to survive. The political organization based on centralism and the military set-up focused on the legions were of no use against the new internal and external threats that were menacing the stability of the Empire. First of all, Diocletian decided to find an alternative to the excessive centralism of the Roman administrative apparatus that had been among the main causes of the ineffective military response to the invasions and the secessions of Gaul and Palmyra. He then gradually developed the innovative system known as the Tetrarchy, which was created with the main aim of avoiding succession wars when an emperor died. The dynastic system of succession having proved totally inadequate for the new times, Diocletian started to determine imperial succession according to the adoption principle. Each ruling emperor was now to choose his own heir soon after assuming power, in order to avoid internecine conflicts. Future emperors were now chosen according to their personal valour and military virtues, for the benefit of the Roman state. Additionally, the whole Empire was divided into four parts, ruled by two senior emperors and two junior emperors. Each senior emperor, known as the Augustus, controlled one half of the Empire; he also elected his own successor, who was known as the Caesar (junior emperor). Each half of the Empire was divided into two parts: one ruled by the Augustus and one by the Caesar. While the senior emperor exerted some formal control over his junior colleague, the Empire was effectively divided into four smaller sub-empires, each having autonomous administrative structures.

The Tetrarchy of Diocletian was a very intelligent response to various political problems, primarily that of succession. When an Augustus died or retired, the Caesar whom he had chosen took his place and nominated a new junior emperor, essentially eliminating the need for civil wars. Similarly, the problem of secessions had been practically cancelled. Each of the four parts of the Empire had its own supreme leader and administrative apparatus, augmenting the efficiency of defence in case of foreign invasion. The old administrative division based on provinces was abolished, being substituted by a new system that saw the organization of the territory into twelve dioceses. The four parts of the Empire ruled by the tetrarchs were known as praetorian prefectures, each of which comprised three dioceses. All these changes greatly simplified the internal organization of the Empire, especially militarily, with flexibility and adaptability being the key elements for success and the only way

Roman heavy infantryman from the Late Empire equipped with spear and round shield. (*Photo by Rachele Lori, copyright by Protectores Domini Nostri & Romars*)

Roman officer from the Late Empire wearing a helmet of the spangenhelm model. (*Photo by Rachele Lori, copyright by Protectores Domini Nostri*)

to face multiple threats. Each of the dioceses was ruled by a governor known as a *vicarius*, while each praetorian prefecture was governed by an Augustus or Caesar with the important support of a chief of staff known as a *praefectus praetorio*. From a military point of view, the reforms of Diocletian were revolutionary and proved highly effective. First of all, he separated in a definitive way the military apparatus from the administrative set-up: he did this in all sectors of the state, from the lowest one to the top of the imperial command structure. For centuries, the senatorial class had controlled both the military and civil administrations, but the specific needs of the new times had revealed the deficiencies of this system. Both the Roman Army and the civil administration now required high levels of specialization, which forced Diocletian to create separate careers and training activities. The military was now in the hands of the *equites*, who had been in command of all the major units for several decades, whereas the civil administration remained under the control of the senatorial class, which now had more specific economic and social functions.

Being a veteran military commander of humble origins, together with his loyal co-emperor Maximian, Diocletian stabilized the frontiers without conducting any major military campaigns. Diocletian ruled over the eastern portion of the Empire and thus faced the Sassanids, while Maximian ruled over the western part and fought against the Germanic peoples. In AD 293, according to the new system of the Tetrarchy, both Diocletian and Maximian appointed their junior emperors, who were – respectively – Galerius and Constantius Clorus. While Galerius was defeated by the Sassanids, Constantius Clorus obtained some significant victories over the Picts in Britain. In AD 305, Diocletian and Maximian jointly abdicated and retired, thereby elevating Galerius and Constantius Clorus to the rank of senior emperors. They soon appointed their own junior emperors: Maximinus Daza in the eastern territories for Galerius, and Severus in western lands for Constantius Clorus. In AD 306, however, Constantius Clorus died in York while on campaign. This caused the first significant problems for the new system of the Tetrarchy, as rather than accepting the elevation of Severus from junior to senior emperor, the Roman legions in Britannia proclaimed Constantius Clorus' son – Constantine – as new senior emperor. Galerius tried to avoid the outbreak of a civil war between Severus and Constantine by assigning the position of senior emperor to Severus and that of junior emperor to Constantine. This act by Galerius temporarily avoided the outbreak of a civil war, but was interpreted – correctly – as a violation of the Tetrarchy's rules by Maxentius, the son of Maximian. Maxentius declared himself emperor at Rome in AD 306, initiating what became known as the Civil Wars of the Tetrarchy. Severus moved against Rome from his capital of Mediolanum, at the head of the army that had previously been commanded by Maximian. However, when Severus besieged Rome, his troops

Roman heavy infantryman from the Late Empire equipped with ridge helmet and scale armour.
(Photo by Rachele Lori, copyright by Protectores Domini Nostri)

deserted to Maxentius. Severus was forced to surrender and Maxentius started to rule the Italian Peninsula jointly with his father, Maximian, who returned to active political life. In AD 307, Galerius marched to Italy at the head of a large army, but his invasion ended in failure, Maxentius being able to win the loyalty of his opponent's soldiers and convince them to mutiny. Galerius, defeated, was forced to go back to the East.

Following these events, Maximian tried to establish an alliance with Constantine and arranged the marriage of him with his daughter, Fausta. In AD 308, relations between Maximian and his son, Maxentius, changed dramatically when the former unsuccessfully tried to eliminate his direct heir. At this point, the elderly Maximian fled north and joined Constantine, in search of an ally who could defeat Maxentius. Shortly after these events, Licinius was appointed by Galerius as the new senior

Roman heavy infantryman from the Late Empire wearing a *manica* for protection of the right forearm and metal greaves. (*Photo by Rachele Lori, copyright by Protectores Domini Nostri*)

emperor in the West and was ordered to swiftly defeat the usurper Maxentius. In AD 310, Maximian rebelled against his protector Constantine, attempting to launch a mutiny of his troops, but he was soon defeated and captured by Constantine, who moved against Maximian after suspending his operations against the Franks. Maximian died shortly afterwards, having been encouraged to commit suicide by Constantine. In AD 311, Galerius died, destroying what little stability remained in the Tetrarchy. Soon thereafter, Maximinus Daza and Licinius began fighting for dominance over the eastern part of the Roman Empire. Meanwhile, Maxentius mobilized his forces for a direct confrontation with Constantine. During the winter of AD 311–312, Constantine, a skilled diplomat as well as a brilliant military commander, forged a strong alliance with Licinius by organizing his marriage to his sister, Constantia. In response to these moves, Maximinus Daza allied himself with Maxentius and sent some of his troops to Italy. Constantine then prepared a pre-emptive attack on Maxentius, which materialized in the spring of AD 312 when he crossed the Alps at the head of 40,000 soldiers. Maxentius tried to slow down the advance of his enemy by sending his cavalry to northern Italy, but they were routed by Constantine, who moved rapidly to occupy the strategically important city of Mediolanum. Maxentius' forces were in very strong defensive positions around present-day Verona, but Constantine was eventually able to overcome them. The invaders also occupied other vital centres in northern Italy, such as Aquileia and Ravenna.

Thanks to his brilliant military successes in northern Italy, Constantine was able to enter central Italy and march on Rome. Maxentius prepared himself for a siege of Rome, counting on the loyalty of the Praetorian Guard and the city being well-stocked with African grain. The capital of the Empire was surrounded by the recently built and seemingly impregnable Aurelian Walls, meaning it would have been very difficult for Constantine to storm the city. Maxentius ordered the destruction of all the bridges that crossed the Tiber and built a single pontoon bridge across the river. While Constantine marched across central Italy, however, Maxentius was forced to change his strategy due to the increasing malcontent of Rome's inhabitants. Realizing that in the event of a siege the population would have revolted against his rule and sided with Constantine, he decided to assemble all his forces and move against his rival in order to fight a decisive pitched battle. The battle took place not far from the new pontoon bridge – known as the Milvian Bridge – that Maxentius had recently built. On paper, Maxentius could count on an army that was much larger than that of his rival, but Constantine's troops consisted of battle-hardened veterans. In addition, Constantine boosted the morale of his men by giving them a new insignia with the *Chi-Rho* Christian symbol shortly before the battle. According to legend, Constantine

Roman heavy infantryman from the Late Empire equipped with ridge helmet and scale armour.
(*Photo by Rachele Lori, copyright by Protectores Domini Nostri*)

Roman light infantryman from the Late Empire equipped with javelin and round shield.
(Photo by Rachele Lori, copyright by Protectores Domini Nostri & Romars)

was visited by a dream the night before the battle and was advised to adopt such a symbol in order to achieve victory; in the dream, Constantine was told the famous expression '*In Hoc Signo Vinces*', or 'Win By This Symbol'). The Greek letters *Chi* (X) and *Rho* (P) were the first two letters of the Greek spelling of the word 'Christ'; together they were used as a common Christian symbol, so Constantine's decision to have them on his new insignia had a very clear religious meaning. Before facing his enemy in a decisive engagement, Constantine embraced the Christian fate. His conversion was perceived as an example to follow by many of his soldiers, marking the beginning of a new era in Roman history. If Constantine prevailed in the coming battle, the Christian faith would be recognized as a legitimate religion of the Roman Empire, having been persecuted for centuries, especially under Diocletian, who was responsible for the murder of thousands of Christians.

Ideologically, the Battle of the Milvian Bridge thus became a clash between the new champion of the Christians (Constantine) and the last defender of paganism (Maxentius). The Battle of the Milvian Bridge began with a charge by Constantine's cavalry, which rapidly destroyed the mounted forces of Maxentius. After this initial success, Constantine ordered a general advance of his infantry. His battle-hardened veterans, thanks to their superior training and discipline, crushed the enemy lines with a single charge and pushed many of Maxentius' soldiers into the Tiber, where they were killed or drowned. The Praetorians were the only soldiers of Maxentius who maintained their position, but after being charged by the cavalry of Constantine they too broke ranks and fled to the river. Maxentius, seeing that the battle was lost, attempted to cross the Milvian Bridge in order to reach Rome, but was pushed into the Tiber by the mass of his fleeing soldiers and drowned. Constantine's victory was complete: he was met with popular jubilation upon his entrance in Rome and secured control over the whole of Italy. To win the loyalty of the African territories, who had originally sided with Maxentius, he sent the head of his rival to Carthage. Fearing invasion by the new master of Rome, the military commanders in Africa joined Constantine's cause.

While these events took place in the Western Empire, Maximinus Daza and Licinius confronted each other in the East. Maximinus Daza exerted his control over the Asiatic territories, while Licinius held power in the Balkans. In AD 313, Maximinus Daza left Syria at the head of 70,000 soldiers and reached Anatolia, with the objective of landing in the Balkans. However, harsh weather he encountered along the way severely weakened his army, giving some precious time to Licinius. In April AD 313, Maximinus Daza crossed the Bosporus and went to Byzantium, one of Licinius' strongholds. The city was taken after a brief siege, as was Heraclea a few days later. Licinius, having assembled an army of 30,000 men, moved against his rival not far from Heraclea. The decisive clash of the campaign took place at Tzirallum and – against all odds – ended with a clear victory for Licinius. The defeated Maximinus Daza had to halt his invasion of the Balkans and return to his Asiatic lands. He tried to stop Licinius' advance at the Cilician Gates, a strategic system of mountain passes that connected southern Anatolia with northern Syria. Licinius, however, broke through the hastily prepared defences of his opponent and forced him to retreat to Tarsus. Maximinus Daza then died, probably of natural causes, although some contemporaries suggested that he had been poisoned. This led to the end of hostilities and left Licinius as the only ruler of the eastern half of the Roman Empire.

By late AD 313, a confrontation between the forces of Constantine and Licinius seemed inevitable, both leaders being determined to end the political system of the Tetrarchy and thus reunify the Empire under his control. For some years, however, both monarchs reorganized their armies and consolidated their power. In AD 313, before Licinius could assume complete control in the East, they had met in Milan (Mediolanum) to confirm an alliance between themselves and agreed to enact the Edict of Milan. This, for the first time in Roman history, officially granted tolerance to Christianity and all the other religions of the Empire. It repudiated any form of religious coercion and greatly favoured the spread of the Christian faith. Nevertheless, hostilities eventually broke out between Constantine and Licinius in AD 316. The new war began with a massive offensive by Constantine in the Balkans, where Licinius, being greatly outnumbered, had no choice but to fall back in good order. Licinius inflicted significant losses on his opponent and prevented the disintegration of his own army. Constantine's offensive started with a significant victory in Pannonia, at the Battle of Cibalae, but he was unable to destroy Licinius' forces. After months of campaigning in the Balkans, another major clash took place at Mardia in Thrace. This proved extremely bloody for both sides and once more ended in an indecisive victory for Constantine, Licinius being able to avoid capture and escape with a large portion of his troops. At this point, with both sides exhausted, they decided to suspend hostilities and sign a peace treaty. According to the peace terms that were agreed in March AD 317, Licinius ceded to Constantine all his Balkan territories except for Thrace. The years that followed were spent by both emperors in preparation for a new war, one which would prove decisive for the destiny of the Roman world.

In AD 320, Licinius reneged on the religious freedom promised by the Edict of Milan and resumed the persecution of Christians in his territories. These acts were perceived as a challenge by Constantine, who was determined to use Christianity as an innovative social element that could help the survival of the Roman Empire. In AD 324, hostilities between Constantine and Licinius resumed. Constantine moved against his rival's defensive positions on the frontier of Thrace and the first significant

Roman archers from the Late Empire. The figure on the left is wearing a corselet of scale armour.
(*Photo by Rachele Lori, copyright by Protectores Domini Nostri*)

Roman officer from the Late Empire wearing a *pileus pannonicus* cap made of fur. (*Photo by Rachele Lori, copyright by Protectores Domini Nostri*)

engagement of the new conflict was fought at Adrianople. This ended in victory for Constantine, who thus expelled Licinius from his last territorial possession in Europe and conquered Thrace. The Battle of Adrianople was a gigantic clash, with 130,000 soldiers of Constantine facing 160,000 men of Licinius. Both armies comprised significant numbers of Germanic warriors, Constantine having allied himself with the Franks and Licinius linking up with the Goths. Before crossing the sea to invade Asia, Constantine had to send his fleet against that of Licinius. In the ensuing Battle of the Hellespont, one of the largest naval clashes of Antiquity, Licinius' fleet – despite its numerical superiority – was completely destroyed. Following this success, Constantine seized the strategic city of Byzantium and landed in Anatolia. He then marched towards Chalcedon, in preparation for the pitched battle that would determine the outcome of the war. On 18 September AD 324, the decisive Battle of Chrysopolis began with a massive frontal attack launched by Constantine, which rapidly routed most of Licinius' troops. Constantine's soldiers killed around 30,000 of their opponents, destroying the combat capability of Licinius. Fleeing to the city of Nicomedia, Licinius finally surrendering to Constantine on the promise that his life would be spared. Constantine accepted such terms and permitted Licinius to live as a private citizen. However, in AD 325, Constantine accused his old rival of plotting against his rule and had him executed. The death of Licinius left Constantine – who was later nicknamed Constantine the Great – as the sole ruler of the reunified Roman Empire. With the civil wars of the Tetrarchy having ended, the new historical phase known as the Late Empire had officially begun. Constantine's reign saw the consolidation of the Empire's borders, the emperor repulsing the Goths north of the Danube and even planning to conduct a major invasion of the Sassanid Empire. Before this could materialize, however, he died of natural causes in AD 337. Following his death, the Roman Empire was partitioned between his three sons – Constantine II, Constantius and Constans – until AD 350.

Chapter 2

The Late Roman Army

Gallienus, who ruled the Roman Empire from AD 260–268, is commonly considered as the first Roman emperor who realized that the military organization created by Augustus had to be completely changed in order for it to more effectively defend the Empire. The traditional structure consisting of legions and *auxilia* units was too static to counter the massive migrations of Germanic peoples or the large-scale invasions of the Sassanids. In addition, civil unrest and internal threats had to be taken into consideration. Until the beginning of the Crisis of the Third Century, the Roman Army had only been employed to fight on the frontiers, but the experiences of the civil wars had clearly shown the need to use the armed forces to also perform police functions. One of the consequences of the Crisis of the Third Century had been the birth of a new phenomenon of internal unrest, a brigandage that saw the formation of large bands of insurgents/criminals (commonly known as *Bagaudes*). As a result, the army had to be ready to maintain public order in addition to serving on the frontiers. Gallienus tried to resolve all these problems, starting with the defence of the frontiers. The idea of a static line of defence had been totally surpassed by events: the Empire now needed central reserves of highly mobile troops, which could move very rapidly to deal with different menaces in several points of the *limes*. The only units that could display such levels of mobility were the cavalry, as the legionary or auxiliary infantry garrisoned on the borders were unable to react against simultaneous threats. Initially, Gallienus created four small cavalry reserves, located in strategic places of the Empire: Mediolanum in northern Italy, Sirmium in Serbia, Poetovio in Slovenia and Lychnidos in Macedonia. Over time, those at Mediolanum and Sirmium became the most important, where large strategic reserves of cavalry were stationed. The troops in Mediolanum were ready to deal with any emergency threatening Italy, while those in Sirmium could act on the long Danubian *limes*.

As a result of Gallienus' cavalry reforms, mounted units quickly became much more important than before. The Romans had never considered cavalry a vital part of their armies, but the Constitutio Antoniana had transformed all provincials into Roman citizens so new cavalry units could now be easily recruited in all the provinces of the Empire. The collapse of the *auxilia* system and the simultaneous expansion of the cavalry led to the birth of several new categories of mounted troops, which made

Pictish warlord. (*Colour plate by Patricio Greve Moller, copyright of Gabriele Esposito*)

Pictish warrior armed with throwing javelins and square-shaped shield.
(*Photo and copyright by Julien Danielo, historical reconstruction by Letavia*)

up the new strategic reserves and had some innovative characteristics. The reforms of Gallienus mostly affected the leadership of the army, with the senatorial class formally excluded from any form of military service. The aristocracy, which for centuries had controlled the entire Roman military machine, was in such a state of decay that the emperor assigned command of the whole military apparatus to the richest members of the *equites*. Gallienus' actions were not revolutionary, merely transforming an informal practice into a formal one. Since the time of Marcus Aurelius, senators had gradually and voluntarily abandoned the role of the legions' commanders, preferring to dedicate themselves to more lucrative activities such as trading. The traditional ethos of the Roman aristocrats had disappeared, together with the ancestral values of Roman society. Fortunately for Rome, however, this important heritage was accepted by the equestrians of the new *honestiores* social class, who were ready to take the place of the senators in the ranks of the army. The *Legatus Legionis* was thus replaced by the *Praefectus Legionis*, who was a member of the *equites*. The general expansion of cavalry was not limited to the creation of new separate mounted units, but also involved the transformation of legionary cavalry. Since the rule of Augustus, the cavalry of each legion consisted of just 120 horsemen, divided into four *turmae* with thirty soldiers each. Now, under the reforms of Gallienus, each legion's cavalry was expanded with the establishment of an *ala miliaria*, comprising twenty-four *turmae* of thirty men, for a total of 720 horsemen.

The Roman military reforms of the third century were not limited to the cavalry; the legionary infantry were also deeply affected by them, especially regarding light troops. The Roman Army had employed provincial soldiers to form the majority of its light infantry units, and the legions had always comprised a number of lightly equipped infantrymen. These were known as *antesignani*, which can be traced back to the times of Julius Caesar. Basically, the *antesignani* were elite light infantry who made up the vanguard of each legion. They were frequently used for special missions and carried lighter equipment than the normal heavy infantry legionaries. They were not part of the heavy infantry formations, and used small oval shields instead of the large ones carried by standard legionaries. During marches, their main functions were to explore the surrounding area and protect the flanks of the legion. In battle, they dealt with enemy missile troops and supported cavalry attacks thanks to their superior mobility. Yet despite their important functions, the *antesignani* were not a separate corps within the legions. They were not a standing unit, but were drawn from the ranks of the regular cohorts when tactical considerations demanded it. Their assignments, albeit very important, were always temporary. The *antesignani* were usually the youngest and fittest legionaries of each cohort, as they performed special missions that needed a high level of mobility. During the third century, in particular under the reign of Septimius Severus, the light infantry component of the legions started to be increasingly important and acquired a stable organization. Apparently, the first legions to have a fixed number of light infantrymen, who performed as skirmishers on a permanent basis, were the three new ones created by Septimius Severus for his Parthian campaign. Since their first encounters with the Parthian mounted archers, the Romans had clearly suffered from a lack of missile troops in their heavy infantry formations. It appears that Septimius Severus tried to resolve this problem by including a fixed number of light infantrymen in his three newly raised elite legions. According to the new structure introduced for these formations, and later adopted by all the legions, each cohort was to include two centuries of light infantry and four of heavy infantry (the elite *Cohors Prima* had two centuries of light infantry and three of heavy infantry). The transformation of two centuries from heavy to light infantry reveals the increasing need for missile troops.

After triumphing at the Battle of the Milvian Bridge, Constantine initiated a complete transformation of the whole Roman Army. The basic idea behind this general reform was to create a new fundamental distinction between military units, with the field armies separated from the border troops. The field armies were garrisoned in the major cities of the Empire, acting as highly mobile strategic reserves, while the border troops were based along the *limes*, serving as the first line of defence against foreign attacks. In practice, the reforms were based on the principle of defence in depth. In case of simultaneous attacks on various points of the border, the frontier troops were to stop the enemies for just a few hours or days; in the meantime, the field armies would be rapidly assembled and sent against the invaders. This new system had a great advantage in that the presence of field armies in the major cities of the Empire boosted the internal security of various territories, these elite troops being available to crush any rebellions or secessions. By the time of Constantine, internal stability was as important to the Empire as defence against foreign invasions. All units of the Roman Army were now divided into two categories: the *comitatenses* (field troops) and the *limitanei* (border troops). In many respects, the *comitatenses* were the direct heirs of the former legions, while the *limitanei* had some characteristics in common with the previous auxiliaries. The *comitatenses* were all the units that made up a field army, known as a *comitatus*, whereas the *limitanei* comprised all the units stationed on the border (*limes*). The former were elite troops with excellent equipment and training, mostly legions or cavalry *vexillationes* (detachments); the latter were organized into smaller units with a strong local character, usually showing a high degree of foreign influence.

The *limitanei* were obviously much more static than the *comitatenses*, being strongly linked to the defensive positions that they had to protect (they were a mix between border police and garrison militia). The *limitanei* were designed to counter small-

Pictish warrior armed with spear and square-shaped shield.
(*Photo and copyright by Julien Danielo, historical reconstruction by Letavia*)

scale enemy incursions or skirmishing activities. Most Roman border regions were characterized by an endemic state of low-intensity conflict, which the *limitanei* were prepared to face on a daily basis. In most cases, the *limitanei* had lighter equipment than the *comitatenses* and enjoyed fewer privileges (such as tax exemptions) than the field troops. However, at the end of their service they received some land located near the border that they had defended for most of their lives. It is possible to suppose that

Pictish warrior armed with axe and round shield. (*Colour plate by Patricio Greve Moller, copyright of Gabriele Esposito*)

Constantine wanted to create a whole new class of military settlers, with the *limitanei* being defenders of the frontiers and having strong personal links to the border lands of the Empire. This view is confirmed by the fact that by the time of Constantine's ascendancy, the profession of soldier had become mostly hereditary in the Roman Empire, so members of the *limitanei* would pass their land properties to their sons and protection of the borders would be guaranteed by these 'military families'. According to their specific function, the *limitanei* could assume some special denominations. If they were stationed on the Rhine or Danubian frontiers, they were commonly known as *riparienses* (their tract of frontier being marked by rivers); if they were garrisoned in large border forts, they were known as *castellani*; if they were placed in smaller forts or watchtowers, they went under the name *burgarii*. In certain cases, for example during a military emergency or for a large-scale campaign, some units of *limitanei* could be attached to the *comitatenses*. In such circumstances they received the denomination of *pseudocomitatenses*; their period of service with the field armies was generally quite limited, but on some occasions the best units of *pseudocomitatenses* could remain attached to the field troops indefinitely.

The *comitatenses* were grouped into several field armies, which were deployed across the Empire. There was, however, a special category of field army: the *comitatus praesentalis* (literally 'the army in the imperial presence'). The *comitatus praesentalis* was the emperor's own field army, which was under his direct control; each of the other field armies was commanded by a high officer known as a *magister militum*, who was assisted by a *magister peditum* (commander of the infantry) and *magister equitum* (commander of the cavalry). As time progressed, the *comitatus praesentalis* started to be commanded by a *magister militum* like all the other field armies. Smaller field armies, instead, were now commanded by a high officer known as a *comes*, while all the *limitanei* of a certain border region were under the command of a *dux*. Both the *comes* and the *dux* were subordinates to the *magister militum*. The most senior units of the *comitatenses* field armies were known as *palatini*; they could be legions, cavalry *vexillationes* or *auxilia palatina*. The latter were elite light infantry units created by Constantine by converting the semi-regular corps of Germanic warriors into proper regular corps. The *auxilia palatina* were generally named after the barbarian tribe from which they had been recruited, but some could be named after the emperor who had organized them. Over time, the Roman forces reformed by Constantine started to include an increasing number of irregular military units of Germanic warriors. Generally speaking, the foreign irregulars serving in the Roman Army could belong to three different categories: the *buccellarii* (mercenaries), the *laeti* (settler soldiers) and the *foederati* (allies). After the defeat of Adrianople by the Goths, many leading Roman military commanders started to expand the forces under their command by

Pictish warrior armed with sword and axe. Tattoos were a typical element of the Picts' tribal culture.
(*Colour plate by Patricio Greve Moller, copyright of Gabriele Esposito*)

Pictish archer armed with bow and knife.
(*Colour plate by Patricio Greve Moller, copyright of Gabriele Esposito*)

forming large contingents of Germanic mercenaries. These soldiers were recruited singularly or in groups and were assembled into units that were under the direct orders of their employers. More or less each *magister militum* started to have several units of mercenaries among his forces. These Germanic troops, paid directly by their employer, generally proved to be very loyal towards the various Roman senior officers but had no loyalty to the emperor or the central administration of the state. In practical terms, several private armies had thus sprung up within the Roman Empire.

The use of *buccellarii* gradually became more widespread, and many Roman nobles, especially in the provinces, started to assemble security forces made up of Germanic mercenaries. As the central state was in great difficulty, many rich landowners preferred to use foreign professional soldiers to protect their own private properties. The term *buccellarii* derives from the word *buccellatum*, a type of dry biscuit that was the ordinary ration of the Germanic mercenaries. Sometimes the private bodyguards could be converted into regular military units, such as the *Placidi Valentiniaci felices*, who were originally recruited as *buccellarii* by Empress Galla Placidia before being converted into an *auxilia palatina*. The units of *buccellarii* did not have a proper military organization, but during the later years of the Empire they became better trained and equipped than many regular units. If at the service of a rich general or noble, they were more motivated than regular soldiers. The term *laeti* defines communities of barbarians that were permitted to settle on imperial territory in exchange for military service in the Roman Army. Initially this recruiting system was used with defeated tribes, which were absorbed into the Empire. The first *laeti* communities appeared during the reign of Marcus Aurelius, who granted some lands to the Germanic tribes defeated during the Marcomannic Wars; the Antonine Plague had depopulated large areas of the Empire, greatly reducing the traditional recruiting potential of Rome. This first experiment of Marcus Aurelius, however, was not a great success, the defeated Germanic warriors soon rising up in revolt and even seizing for a brief period the important city of Ravenna. Each community of barbarians that wished to enter imperial territory had to conclude an agreement with the Roman authorities, which prescribed a series of obligations but sometimes also privileges. The agreement granting land to a community of barbarians might specify a once-and-for-all contribution of recruits or a fixed number of recruits required each year. The lands given to Germanic settlers were known as *terrae laeticae* and were not part of the normal provincial administration, since they were under the direct control of a specific military officer (known as *Praefectus Laetorum* or *Praefectus Gentilium*). There is still considerable dispute among scholars about the military organization of the *laeti*, it being unclear if these barbarian recruits formed their own distinct military formations or if they were simply absorbed into existing units. The second hypothesis, however, seems to be the most plausible, with the *Praefecti Laetorum* just administrative officers controlling the communities of foreign settlers, but having no units of barbarians under their command. *Foederati*, instead, were all those tribes that were allied to Rome due to the terms of a treaty (known as a *foedus*). Generally speaking, tribes of *foederati* were provided with benefits by Rome in exchange for military assistance. Their loyalty towards the Empire, however, was not very sincere. Indeed, most of the early *foederati*, like the Franks or the Goths, later transformed themselves into fully independent barbarian nations located within Roman territories. On some rare occasions, military collaboration between Rome and its Germanic allies

had positive results. In most cases, however, the Germanic tribes only accepted a *foedus* to enter the Roman Empire and then create their own independent realm. From an organizational point of view, the contingents of *foederati* were commanded by their own leaders and retained their peculiar military traditions.

During the Early Empire, both legionaries and auxiliaries were all *voluntarii* (volunteers). Compulsory military conscription did exist in the Roman world, but was used only very rarely. The practice of conscription, which was known as *dilectus*, was employed only in case of military emergencies or during the preparation of major campaigns for which large numbers of additional troops were required. This situation changed completely after the Crisis of the Third Century: by the time of Constantine, in fact, the Roman Army relied mainly on compulsion for the recruitment of citizens. As we have seen, the reforms of Diocletian made military professions hereditary, with the sons of serving soldiers or veterans required by law to enlist in order to continue the service of their fathers. Furthermore, all citizens of the Empire were subject to a regular annual levy based on a principle known as *indictio* (a sort of land tax assessment). Each landowner living on the territory of the Empire was required to provide a certain number of recruits to the imperial army, this number being defined according to the amount of land tax that was due on each landowner's estates. This second channel of recruitment was strongly opposed

Pictish heavy cavalryman wearing scale armour. (*Colour plate by Patricio Greve Moller, copyright of Gabriele Esposito*)

Pictish light cavalryman playing a horn.
(*Colour plate by Patricio Greve Moller, copyright of Gabriele Esposito*)

by the rich landowners, who preferred to keep their best men on their estates (for work or for their private defence). In order to replace their best men, landowners often sent the less fit or reliable men at their disposal; as an alternative, they could cheat the authorities by sending sons of soldiers (who were already obliged to serve) or vagabonds (known as *vagi*). The principle of *indictio* could only be used in the countryside, it mostly involving peasant recruits and affecting the local power of the various landowners. In the urban centres, this land-based conscription could not be applied. Consequently, cities provided little to the defence of the Empire. Landowners were also frequently able to convert the conscription requirements into a cash levy (with a fixed rate per recruit due). This was known as *aureum tironicum*, from the word *tirones*, meaning 'recruits'. During the Middle Empire, the traditional height and age requirements were progressively abandoned, with the result that the general quality of soldiers saw a dramatic decline. After being accepted into the Roman Army, each new recruit was marked on one of his arms with a specific brand. This was done in order to discourage desertion, which became an enormous problem during the closing decades of the Western Empire. Each new recruit was issued with an identification disk that was worn around the neck, and was also given a certificate of enlistment that was known as *probatoria*. Unsurprisingly, the best recruits were generally assigned to the *comitatenses*, while the men having an inferior level of fitness ended up in the static units of *limitanei*. The standard period of service was twenty years in the *comitatenses* and twenty-four years in the *limitanei*, which had changed only little from the time of legionaries and *auxilia*.

All the difficulties related to recruiting described above had obvious consequences on the strength of individual units, which became notably smaller than previously, especially the legions. There was always a massive disparity between official and actual strengths, with units in the field generally much smaller than their theoretical establishment. With the great military reforms of Constantine, the legion remained the basic unit of the Roman infantry, although its internal composition was greatly changed. Until the Crisis of the Third Century, the legions had acted more or less as independent small armies, having their own cavalry and artillery. However, after the organizational reforms of Diocletian and Constantine, they lost this peculiar character and their numerical strength was notably reduced. Most of the legions created or reorganized by Diocletian and Constantine derived from former *vexillationes* (detachments of legions), each having an average of between 1,000 and 1,200 soldiers. The new legion of the Roman Army was commanded by a *Tribunus* coming from the equestrian class. He was assisted by the *Primicerius*, his second-in-command, the term being a new version of the old *Primus Pilus*. The *Primicerius* was an ex-ranker with considerable length of service, who had entered the officer corps due to his experience in combat. The previous internal organization of cohorts was completely abandoned, each legion now structured on six *ordines*, each of which included two centuries of legionaries. Each *ordo* thus numbered 200 men, meaning the whole legion had some 1,200 soldiers. Each *ordo* was commanded by an officer known as a *Ducenarius*, who could also be known as a senator. Despite its denomination, the rank of senator had nothing to do with the senatorial class. The first *centuria* of each *ordo* was commanded by the *Ducenarius*, while the second one was under the orders of a *Centenarius* (the equivalent of the former centurion). Both the *Ducenarius* and the *Centenarius* appointed their own adjutant and second-in-command, who was called a *Biarchus*. These performed more or less the same functions as the former *Optio*, including remaining at the back of the century in order to maintain its formation. As previously, each century was structured on ten *contubernia*, and each *contubernium* was now commanded by an NCO known as a *Semissalis*, the equivalent of the old *Decanus*.

The majority of the legions were part of the *comitatenses* troops, but some of them were *limitanei*. The *auxilia palatina*, elite units of light infantry, generally performed special duties and had their own peculiar equipment. Their organization was similar to that of the heavy infantry legions, but they numbered only 500–600 men each. Each *auxilia palatina* included just three *ordines*, with two centuries each. The chain of command and internal organization of each *ordo* were exactly the same as in the legions. The majority of the *auxilia palatina* comprised light infantrymen armed with small shields and javelins, but there is evidence of some units entirely formed of foot archers. Most of the *limitanei* units were structured as independent cohorts or as *numeri*. The cohort of Constantine's Roman Army included six centuries of eighty men each, for a total of 480 troops. Each cohort was commanded by a *Tribunus*, who was assisted by a *Primicerius*, as in the legions. Each century was under the orders of an *Ordinarius*, the equivalent of the *Ducenarius* or *Centenarius* from the legions (although he had fewer privileges). Each *Ordinarius* was assisted by a *Biarchus* and commanded ten *contubernia*. The *numeri*, units mostly composed of barbarians, retained their characteristic 'local' nature as part of the *limitanei*, being organized on eight centuries with eighty men each (a total of 640 soldiers). Each *numerus* was commanded by a *Tribunus*, who had a *Primicerius* as his deputy. The eight centuries of each *numerus* were assembled into four *ordines*, each of which was commanded by a *Ducenarius*. Differently from what happened in a legion, each century of the *numerus* was led by its own *Centenarius*, there being no *Ducenarius* in command of the first century of each *ordo*).

The basic cavalry unit of the *comitatenses* was the *vexillatio*, which initially had the same internal structure as the light infantry *auxilia palatina*. It included between

Scot warlord. (*Colour plate by Patricio Greve Moller, copyright of Gabriele Esposito*)

Scot heavy infantryman equipped with oval shield.
(*Colour plate by Patricio Greve Moller, copyright of Gabriele Esposito*)

500 and 600 cavalrymen, structured on three *ordines* with two centuries each. The chain of command and the internal organization of each *ordo* were exactly the same as in the legions. Over time, each cavalry *vexillatio* started to number just 300 men, meaning the internal organization had to be changed: each unit now included ten *turmae* of thirty men. Each *vexillatio* was commanded by a Tribunus. There were two kinds of units in the cavalry of the *limitanei*: the *alae* and the *cunei*. While the border infantry retained the cohort, the border cavalry preserved the *ala*, which included 600 horsemen and was structured on twenty *turmae* of thirty men each. Each *ala* was commanded by a *Tribunus*. The *cuneus* was originally created as a semi-regular unit of barbarians with no proper internal organization, although it gradually acquired a more stable structure. The *cunei* continued to comprise units of mostly barbarians and retained their characteristic 'local' nature as part of the *limitanei*, but like the *vexillationes* of the *comitatenses* cavalry they started to be organized on ten *turmae* of thirty men. Each *cuneus* was commanded by a *Tribunus*.

Interestingly, during this period of great change the Roman Army started to have some independent artillery units, probably the first military to do so in the history of the world. Prior to the Crisis of the Third Century, each legion deployed its own artillery: each cohort was responsible for a stone-throwing *ballista* and each century had a bolt-shooting *scorpio*. In total, a single Roman legion could deploy an impressive artillery detachment with ten heavy *ballistae* and fifty-nine light *scorpiones*. Around AD 250, the *ballistae* of each cohort started to be replaced by a heavier model of stone-thrower known as the *onager*, a catapult specifically designed for siege operations. The artillery of each legion was manned by a small band of specialists, most of its crews being provided by the ordinary rankers. After the reforms of Constantine, however, this situation was completely changed. The new smaller legions did not have their own artillery detachments, all the legionary artillerymen from the various units instead being assembled together in order to form new and independent artillery legions. The members of these specialized units were known as *ballistarii*. It seems that initially there was just one such specialist legion, which was part of the *comitatenses*. By the early fifth century AD, however, the Roman field armies included six artillery legions: the *Ballistarii seniores*, *Ballistarii iuniores*, *Ballistarii Dafnenses*, *Ballistarii Theodosiaci* and *Ballistarii Theodosiani iuniores* in the Eastern Empire, and the *Ballistarii* in the Western Empire. Only three of these units were of *comitatenses*: the *Ballistarii Dafnenses* and the two original artillery legions (the *Ballistarii seniores* and the *Ballistarii iuniores*). The remaining three artillery units were *pseudocomitatenses* and had been promoted in order to serve with the field armies. It is highly probable that these units were formed by collecting together garrison artillerymen who manned the defensive fortifications located on the *limes*.

Scot medium infantryman equipped with round shield. (*Colour plate by Patricio Greve Moller, copyright of Gabriele Esposito*)

Scot light infantryman equipped with javelins and small round shield.
(*Colour plate by Patricio Greve Moller, copyright of Gabriele Esposito*)

Chapter 3

The Birth of Sub-Roman Britain

During the Late Empire, Britannia was menaced by the Saxons from the south and by the peoples of Scotland from the north. The Scottish tribes had changed a lot since the days of Agricola's campaigns in Caledonia. The various tribal groups had progressively formed a powerful confederation, which initially controlled most of present-day Scotland. The members of this new tribal confederation were called *Picti* by the Romans, since they used to paint their skin with tattoos; as a result, during the Late Empire, the Celtic inhabitants of Scotland became known as Picts. Almost simultaneously with those of Scotland, the Celtic communities of Ireland (called Hibernia by the Romans) also started to form their own large confederation of tribes. Its members were referred to as *Scoti* by the Romans and were quite different from the Picts, having experienced very little direct contact with the Roman Empire. Compared with the Picts, the Scoti or Scots were a people of wild and ferocious warriors who were always in search of new lands to pillage. Differently from the Picts, the Scots had excellent sea-faring capabilities and thus – during the fourth century AD – they started to launch devastating naval raids along the coastline of western Scotland. Soon after the Romans left Britain, in the fifth century, the Scots transformed their incursions into proper attempts at invasion. Over time, thanks to their impressive military skills, they were able to defeat the Picts and occupy a large portion of western Scotland. The Picts had fought for decades against the Roman troops defending Hadrian's Wall, but had never been able to invade and permanently occupy northern England. However, when the Roman legions left Britain and the Scots started to expel the Picts from part of their homeland, the Picts moved south to invade Britannia.

In AD 395, the Roman Empire was definitively divided in two parts: the Western Empire ruled by Emperor Honorius and the Eastern Empire under Emperor Arcadius. The Western Empire soon started to experience great difficulties, coming under pressure from the migrating Germanic confederations that wanted to cross the *limes* of the Rhine. Meanwhile, the Eastern Empire, thanks to its solid economy and strong military resources, was able to repulse attacks from north of the Danube. In the early years of the fifth century, it became apparent that the Roman authorities were no longer capable of defending the vast frontiers of the western half of the

Empire, as too many Germanic groups were on the move and attacking different sectors of the border. The military resources of the Western Empire were too limited numerically to provide an effective response to the crisis, leaving the Romans wit little choice but to abandon some of their territories in order to relocate more troops along the Rhine. The political sphere in Britannia was particularly turbulent during the late fourth and early fifth centuries, with several usurpers rebelling against the central authority of the Empire and seceding – albeit temporarily – from Rome. In total, five major rebellions took place in Britain during the period 350–410, each of which was led by a different usurper: Magnentius (350–353), Magnus Maximus (383–388), Marcus (406), Gratian (407) and Constantine III (407). The geographical isolation of Roman Britain was one of the main factors behind the outbreak of these revolts, the Empire no longer being able to send large armies across the English Channel to crush local rebellions. On most occasions, the usurpers rising to power in Britain were capable warlords, who wanted to become independent from the Empire in order to organize a better defence of their homelands from the attacks of the Picts and the Saxons. Rome had done very little to help Britannia during recent decades, with the local communities starting to feel a sense of abandonment. During the early fifth century, attacks from the north by the Picts became increasingly dangerous, as did naval incursions by the Saxons. Rome was unable to send any reinforcements, and the leading citizens of Britannia were forced to accept the fact that they were no longer under the protection of the Empire.

In AD 402, Stilicho, a Germanic warlord who was overall commander of the Western Empire's forces, transferred several Roman units from Britain to the Continent in order to reinforce the garrison of Gaul. Four years later, the remaining Roman troops in Britannia revolted against the central authorities of the Empire and elected three successive tyrants or usurpers: Marcus, Gratian and Constantine III. The last of these tried to become emperor and went to Gaul with some of his troops, but was decisively defeated during AD 411. As a result of these events, most of the Roman *comitatenses* units had left Britain by AD 410 and had gone to Gaul. The *limitanei* troops, however, remained in Britannia and continued to garrison Hadrian's Wall. In AD 410, Britain effectively ceased to be part of the Roman Empire and became independent, although the country remained part of the Roman cultural world. The Britons spoke Latin, were Christians and identified themselves as Romans: even though their political and military links with the Empire were now severed, their civilization did not change in any dramatic way. It remained a mix of Celtic and Roman elements, which had gradually developed during the previous centuries. The laws and economic institutions of the Britons were clearly Roman, while their material culture and religion were heavily influenced by the ancient Celtic traditions. Consequently,

Scot light infantryman armed with spear, sword and short dagger. (*Colour plate by Patricio Greve Moller, copyright of Gabriele Esposito*)

Scot heavy cavalryman wearing a corselet of chainmail. (*Colour plate by Patricio Greve Moller, copyright of Gabriele Esposito*)

post-410 Britannia is commonly known as Sub-Roman Britain. The former territories of Roman Britain remained united for just a few years after the legions abandoned the island, the various local aristocrats soon starting to create small independent kingdoms based on the pre-Roman Celtic tribal identities. The centralized Roman institutions collapsed quite rapidly, together with the military system of the *limitanei*. This fragmentation of British territory took place in a chaotic age that was characterized by many small-scale civil wars, which weakened the Britons' capability to repulse foreign invasions. In a country that was now dominated by anarchy, no central authority that could effectively oppose the Picts and the Saxons was in existence.

Before AD 410, the Romans had a total of four legions and seventeen cohorts of heavy infantry in Britain, plus a large number of cavalry and locally recruited units. The various corps were under command of three different superior officers: the *Comes Britanniae*, *Comes litoris Saxonici per Britannias* and *Dux Britanniarum*. The *Comes Britanniae* commanded the field army that was stationed in Britannia, while the *Dux Britanniarum* was at the head of the local *limitanei* troops as well as of some *comitatenses* units. The *Comes litoris Saxonici per Britannias* held a peculiar

Scot light cavalryman armed with spear. (*Colour plate by Patricio Greve Moller, copyright of Gabriele Esposito*)

Romano-Briton officer wearing a corselet of scale armour. (*Photo and copyright by Julien Danielo, historical reconstruction by Letavia*)

command that requires specific analysis since it is very important in reconstructing the early Saxon presence in Britain. The *litus Saxonicum*, or 'Saxon Shore', corresponded to the coastal regions of the English Channel. It was divided into two parts: the *litus Saxonicum per Britannias* and the *litus Saxonicum per Gallias*. The *litus Saxonicum per Britannias* consisted of the English coastline, and the *litus Saxonicum per Gallias* the French coastline, each of which had an independent military command with its own *Comes* (count). But why were the coast of the English Channel known as the Saxon Shore, and why did the Romans have specific coastal military commands in that area of the Empire? The answer to these questions is very simple: since the late third century AD, the Germanic tribe of the Saxons had targeted the coastal settlements of the English Channel with devastating sea-borne incursions. To face this new threat, the Romans built a series of interconnected fortifications with strong garrisons, tasked with repulse the raids by the Saxons. Consequently, this network of fortifications started to be known as the Saxon Shore, an expression that was later used to indicate specific areas of southern England and northern France. Since the time of Emperor Claudius, the conqueror of Britannia, the Romans had always deployed a military fleet in the English Channel. This was greatly reduced in size during the Crisis of the Third Century but continued to exist thereafter, operating in collaboration with the garrisons of the Saxon Shore fortifications. These defences were built across a wide area, stretching from present-day Portsmouth in Hampshire to Burgh Castle in Norfolk. It is interesting to note that most of the Roman coastal fortifications were located on the estuaries of navigable rivers. This happened for two main reasons: firstly, the Romans wanted to prevent the seaborne raiders from using the major rivers as waterways; secondly, the fortifications also acted as supply bases for Roman warships operating in the English Channel. For several decades, the defensive system of the Saxon Shore worked well in countering the attacks of the Germanic pirates, who became extremely active during the late fourth century. The Saxons were one of the few Germanic peoples with strong seafaring capabilities.

During the early fifth century, the Britons fought for decades, both among themselves and against the invaders from Scotland, who over time started to include Scots as well as Picts. The many kings or tyrants who dominated Sub-Roman Britain had few military resources at their disposal, so were in no position to fight off the massive offensives organized by the Celts from the north. In AD 429, a major battle took place between the Romano-Britons and a large force of Saxon sea-raiders, which ended in defeat for the Germani. The exact location of this clash is unclear, but it is known that the Britons were led by Germanus of Auxerre, a charismatic bishop who had recently come from Gaul and assumed command of the Britons in their struggle against the Saxons. These years were particularly chaotic for Britain, the politically fragmented small realms of the former Britannia having to face frequent attacks launched by the Picts/Scots as well as the Saxons. The Britons tried to resist and to preserve their independence for many years, forming regional alliance between their relatively weak realms to improve their chances of victory against the invaders. In AD 446, following a general worsening of their situation, the political leaders of Britain made a final appeal to the Western Empire for the Roman Army to come back to fight for their homeland. At that time, the consul Flavius Aetius was the most important warlord of the Western Empire, and it is probable that the appeal – commonly known as the *Gemitus Britannorum*, or 'Groans of the Britons' – was addressed to him. Flavius Aetius, however, was already experiencing serious military difficulties in combating the expansionism of Attila's Huns on the Continent, and thus was in no condition to help the Britons.

According to the ancient historian Gildas, in AD 449 – with a renewed invasion being organized by the Picts and the Scots – the various rulers of Britain met to find a common response to the northern threat to their realms. During this crucial meeting, the political leaders of Britain decided to invite some Germanic communities to their territories and to offer them food supplies in exchange for their military services. Recent combat experience had shown that the Britons were too weak to confront a large-scale invasion by the Picts and the Scots, who had formed a temporary alliance in an attempt to conquer Britain. The practice of hiring Germanic warriors in exchange for various concessions was extremely common during the Late Empire, most of the Roman Army consisting of Germanic individuals who served in its ranks as mercenaries. The Roman authorities could recruit Germanic fighters individually or sign a *foedus* (treaty) with an entire tribal group. The *foedus* worked as a contract, its terms detailing the kind of military service required from the Germani and the benefits they were to receive in exchange for their use in combat. The Germanic warriors chosen by the Britons were the Saxons, who were already very active in the English Channel. The Britons thus had first-hand knowledge of the martial skills of the Saxons, and were sure that they would be able to defeat the northern alliance of Celtic peoples. In AD 449, the Picts launched a devastating invasion of England, raiding lands along the eastern coast. By that time, a new political leader had emerged among the Britons. He was named Vortigern, and was a tyrant or local ruler who had secured control of much of Britain. In order to stop the Pictish incursions that were destroying his realm, Vortigern suggested forming an alliance with the Saxons, who, despite having been defeated in AD 429, had continued to raid southern England and threaten its coastline. In exchange for their help against the Picts, Vortigern offered the Saxons a permanent settlement in south-eastern England, assigning them land on the Isle of Thanet. As a result of this, a first wave of Germanic warriors came to

Romano-Briton officer equipped with a helmet of the ridge model. (*Colour plate by Patricio Greve Moller, copyright of Gabriele Esposito*)

Romano-Briton heavy infantryman armed with spear, heavy javelin and sword. (*Photo and copyright by Julien Danielo, historical reconstruction by Letavia*)

Britain under two mighty warlords: the Saxon brothers Hengest and Horsa. The first Saxon *foederati* who came to Britain were not particularly numerous. They had accepted the *foedus* proposed by the Britons purely for the objective of establishing a first permanent presence in England, intending to use their new allies' military weakness to their advantage. Within a few years the number of Saxons fighting as mercenaries for the Britons increased very rapidly, and when they became strong enough, they started to revolt against their employers. Using as a pretext the inadequacy of their monthly supplies, the Saxons opened hostilities by raiding lands in south-eastern England.

Chapter 4

The Picts and the Scots

Following the consolidation of the Roman presence in Britannia, the various Celtic communities living in Caledonia (present-day Scotland) organized themselves as a loose confederation of tribes. Members of the new tribal confederation were called 'Picti' (meaning 'painted') by the Romans, since they used to paint their skin with tattoos; as a result, during the Late Empire, the Celtic inhabitants of Scotland became known as Picts. They retained their distinct military traditions during the Early Middle Ages, which were essentially Celtic. Pictish military contingents were raised according to tribal/family sub-divisions, being strongly linked to the clan to which they belonged. When the leader of a tribe decided to go to war, all the free men living under his protection had to serve. The farmers/warriors thus left their homes and assembled at the hill fort of their warlord. Some military leaders were powerful and rich enough to be named kings, controlling very large territories. In the event of war mobilization, all the minor aristocrats living on the king's lands had to gather together their tribal contingents and join their overlord to form a royal army. Pictish military organization was strongly influenced by the existing social structures and was based on the solid personal relationships existing between the upper class of the nobles and the large community of peasants and farmers. During raids or incursions conducted against bordering tribes, free men could decide to join their warlord in the hope of looting the enemy's resources, but they were not obliged to abandon their farms. However, in case of full-scale foreign invasions or large expeditions of conquest, all able-bodied free individuals were obliged to fight. A Pictish field army was formed of several different contingents, each led by a noble warlord who commanded his own personal retainers. Some of these could be professional fighters who earned a living as soldiers, but the majority were part-time warriors who served in exchange for protection and benefits. Each warlord commanded a different number of warriors and there were no standard tactical units: a great noble could assemble thousands of men, while a minor one might lead into battle just a few dozens of his followers.

Over time, Pictish armies started to include a larger variety of troop types: the infantry remained the most important component from a numerical point of view, but cavalry (comprising both chariots and horsemen) became increasingly decisive

Romano-Briton heavy infantryman wearing chainmail. The emblem painted on the shield is the monogram of Christ. (*Colour plate by Patricio Greve Moller, copyright of Gabriele Esposito*)

Romano-Briton heavy infantryman wearing chainmail and bronze greaves. (*Photo and copyright by Julien Danielo, historical reconstruction by Letavia*)

in the outcome of battles. The cavalry was entirely provided by the aristocracy: warlords of superior rank were mounted on chariots, while minor nobles fought as simple horsemen. Chariots could be used as mobile platforms during battles, but on numerous occasions they were merely employed to transport nobles on the battlefield. Indeed, the aristocrats preferred to fight on foot when the enemy was deployed in close order. Chariots were effective as mobile platforms only at the beginning of a battle (during the preliminary skirmishes) or when it was over (enabling a defeated enemy to be attacked from the rear). All nobles, either fighting on chariots or on horseback, had heavy personal equipment and wore some form of armour. Each of them was accompanied by one or more servants, driving his war chariot or taking care of his horse. Peasants and farmers made up the infantry. The richest of these would fight in the first lines, wearing their complete personal equipment, while the poorest ones fought as missile troops with only light infantry equipment. The bow was never particularly popular as a light infantry weapon among the Picts, so most of the skirmish troops were armed with throwing javelins or slings. In Early Medieval Scotland, all able-bodied males aged 16–60 could be called to serve in the *exercitus Scoticanus*, or 'common army', which included freemen (most of whom were farmers owning small land properties) as well as *neyfs*, or unfree men. The latter were not slaves, but men who were tied for life to the land where they were born. The *neyfs* could be sold or given away with the land on which they lived and worked, but were not treated as proper slaves.

The Picts were the direct heirs of Britain's centuries-old Celtic traditions, so their military equipment was distinctively Celtic. Helmets and cuirasses were not often worn by the Picts, many of the Pictish foot warriors being equipped as axemen and carrying a simple round shield. Corselets of simple organic materials, such as leather, were worn as a cheap alternative to metal cuirasses. Pictish shields were usually highly decorated. They could be rectangular or square in shape, but they were always quite small. The clothes worn by the Picts were – in most cases – decorated with chequered patterns, which were distinctively Celtic and later gave birth to the famous 'tartan' designs. As we have seen, the Picts derived their name from the practice of painting their bodies with tattoos. These could be extremely complex, having a series of important ritual meanings. Most of the Pictish foot soldiers were equipped as light skirmishers, armed with throwing javelins, usually carried in combination with a thrusting spear. The offensive equipment was often completed by a Celtic short sword. The Picts did not have heavy cavalry to speak of, as only a few of their richest warriors could afford a complete set of armour. During the Roman period, the heavy cavalry of the Picts consisted of war chariots, which greatly impressed the Romans because of their excellent manoeuverability. However, war chariots eventually fell out of use and the importance of cavalry in Pictish armies greatly decreased. The few warriors who made up the small Pictish cavalry were mostly employed as explorers and skirmishers, often carrying horns in order to transmit orders from long distances.

During the whole period AD 410–600, the Picts and Scots played a crucial role in the history of Britain. Their expansionism, for example, was the main cause behind the Britons' decision to invite the Saxons to their lands. Initially, the Picts and Scots fought against each other, the Scots occupying a large portion of Scotland's western coastline (in modern Argyll) that had previously been inhabited by the Picts. By AD 600, the Scots living in Argyll had organized themselves into the Kingdom of Dál Riata, a powerful political entity that continued to exist until AD 730. The Picts controlled most of Scotland throughout this period, and on several occasions allied themselves with the Scots to attack the Britons. Around AD 730, however, the Picts finally conquered the Kingdom of Dál Riata after a series of campaigns, thus absorbing the Scots living outside Ireland. Nevertheless, it should be noted that although the Picts were victorious from a military point of view, the Scots were successful culturally. Indeed, by AD 730, the Picts had been fully 'Gaelicized' by the Scots (who were also known as Gaels). Gaelic culture, which had developed in Ireland during the previous centuries, was thus adopted by the Picts and the term 'Scots' began to indicate all the inhabitants of what the Romans had called Caledonia. The region soon started to be known as Scotland, and a true Scottish identity emerged from the ethnic fusion of the Picts with the Scots. Almost simultaneously with those of Scotland, the Celtic communities in Ireland (called Hibernia by the Romans) started to form their own large confederation of tribes. These were referred to as Scoti by the Romans and were quite different from the Picts, having experienced very little direct contact with the Roman Empire. Compared with the Picts, the Scoti (or Scots) were a people of wild and ferocious warriors, always in search of new lands to pillage. Differently from the Picts, the Scots had excellent seafaring capabilities, and during the fourth century AD they started to launch devastating naval raids along the coastline of western Scotland. Having a sizeable fleet of warships at their disposal, the Scots dominated the Irish Sea for a long period and conducted many seaborne incursions against the Britons. Early Medieval Ireland consisted of several small kingdoms inhabited by the Scots (who were also known as Gaels), each of which was based on tribal units singularly known as *tuath* and consisting of several family groups that had long lived on the same territory. The various family groups could be free (the *soer-chele*) or unfree (the *doer-chele*). The former were dominant within their *tuath*, while the latter had to accept decisions taken by members of the *soer-chele* more or less like vassals.

The leading nobles of the *soer-chele* could be kings of three different categories: *Ri-tuaithe*, king of one *tuath*; *Rui-ri*, king of more than one *tuath*; or *Ri-ruirech*, monarch

Romano-Briton heavy infantryman armed with light javelin and sword. (*Photo and copyright by Julien Danielo, historical reconstruction by Letavia*)

of one of the Irish kingdoms. There also were the High Kings, monarchs of one kingdom who temporarily came to exert a direct or indirect influence over some of the other Irish realms. The title of High King was mostly a ceremonial one, as during the Early Medieval period no Irish king was able to unify the whole of Ireland under his control or to stop the continuous inter-state wars that ravaged Irish communities. In the event of war, all the able-bodied adult males of both the *soer-chele* and the *doer-chele* were to follow their *Ri-tuaithe* or *Rui-ri* in battle; the latter, of course, was obliged to serve under his *Ri-ruirech* when required to do so. The forces fielded by a single *tuath* usually consisted of some 700 warriors, who were assembled into a *buiden*, or band. Each *buiden* consisted of seven 'hundreds', or *cet*. Over time, most Gaelic military units started to consist of 300 warriors each and became known as *tricha cet*. There were no precise time limits for military service, but in most cases it was impossible for a king to raise his forces during autumn or spring because in these periods his subjects had to work in the fields. At the beginning of the Early Middle Ages, the territory of present-day Ireland was fragmented into a series of small princedoms, which were constantly at war with each other. These petty states were the direct heirs of some extremely old tribal traditions, which had changed very little across the centuries. Despite lacking any form of political unity, the Scots became famous for their warlike 'national' spirit.

All able-bodied Gaelic males aged over 14 were expected to serve under their warlord in time of war. According to contemporary sources, all Scot freemen were extremely happy to fight for the defence of their homeland or to raid the

Romano-Briton medium infantryman wearing a crested ridge helmet. (*Colour plate by Patricio Greve Moller, copyright of Gabriele Esposito*)

territories of their local enemies. Military service was more a right than a duty, and the endemic state of war existing in Ireland had greatly improved the combat capabilities of the warriors. They knew their home territories very well and were used to fighting with hit-and-run guerrilla tactics that based their success on high mobility. The Gaelic warriors received no pay for their military service, but could divide among themselves the booty taken from defeated enemies. They were reluctant to fight for long periods outside the borders of their home princedom, so external campaigns usually lasted for a maximum of six weeks. Any freeman incapable of attending military service had to equip and send another individual in his place. Unfree males were usually conscripted only to perform auxiliary duties like building encampments or transporting materials. Each major prince had a retinue of professional soldiers under his direct orders; these, in many cases, were relatives of the warlord who were given sustenance and land by him in exchange for their military service. In most cases, the 'military family' of a minor prince numbered around 120 professional warriors, who were the only Gaelic warriors to have horses. These professional fighters, however, usually dismounted to fight and thus did not perform as true cavalry. They were in essence mounted infantry, using horses only to travel long distances. The Scoti were equipped quite differently from the Picts, their civilization being an updated version of the original Celtic one. Like the Picts, the Scots did not widely employ metal helmets and cuirasses. According to ancestral Celtic traditions, they preferred to fight unarmoured in order to show their courage on the battlefield. Gaelic warfare was dominated by frequent inter-tribal wars that were mostly aimed at stealing cattle, so most Scots warriors were equipped as light skirmishers and enjoyed a high degree of mobility. Being of humble origins, they considered inter-tribal warfare and overseas expeditions as an opportunity to improve their social position. The bow was not a particularly popular weapon in Ireland, being used only by a limited number of warriors. Nonetheless, due to the fact that most of the Scot fighters wore no armour, bows could be very effective in battle. The few warriors who made up the small Scots cavalry were mostly employed as explorers and skirmishers, often equipped with just a simple spear. Most of the Scot spears had heads with peculiar shapes; these were influenced by religious symbolism, which was particularly strong in Celtic Ireland. The legendary figure of the hero Cuchullain emerged in Gaelic Ireland during the Early Middle Ages as part of such religious traditions.

Chapter 5

The Saxon Invasion of Britain

The first ancient source that mentions the Saxons dates back to AD 356, but provides very few details. What is known is that they entered the Rhineland during the early fifth century AD, together with several other Germanic tribes. Thanks to the martial skill of their warriors, the Saxons were able to occupy a good portion of the modern Netherlands, displacing the Salian Franks who had been settled in the region. The Saxons already controlled the North Sea coastline of north-western Germany and the southern part of the Jutland Peninsula in present-day Denmark. Following their westwards expansion, they became one of the most prominent Germanic nations. Unlike most of the other Germanic peoples, the Saxons were skilled seafarers, using ships to conduct effective naval raids. They had learned how to navigate from the Jutland Peninsula across the North Sea, progressively improving the quality of their ships by adopting new methods of construction. Originally, the Saxons wanted to settle in northern areas of Gaul, in present-day Belgium. However, it gradually became apparent that the presence of the Franks (the strongest of all the Germani) would prevent them from expanding towards the fertile regions of northern Gaul. With a population that was experiencing a demographic boom and consequently suffering from a chronic shortage of food, the Saxons were left with little choice but to direct their expansionist ambitions towards Britain. After many decades of raids, the Saxons finally had an opportunity to settle present-day England when the Britons offered them a *foedus*. It should be remembered, however, that only part of their communities moved across the English Channel, with a sizeable number of Saxon groups remaining in north-western Germany and south-western Denmark, even after the Saxons became settled in Britain. The Saxons did not come to Britannia alone, being joined by another two minor Germanic groups: the Angles and the Jutes. The Angles inhabited central Denmark, while the Jutes were from northern Denmark. Like the more powerful Saxons, they were capable of building large fleets of agile warships and were strong warriors. The Germanic communities migrating to Britannia also included some Frisians, who lived in the Netherlands on territory that bordered with Saxon lands.

As mentioned in a previous chapter, the Saxons and the other Germanic communities associated with them arrived in Britain as mercenaries, invited to do

Romano-Briton medium infantryman armed with spear. (*Photo and copyright by Julien Danielo, historical reconstruction by Letavia*)

Romano-Briton medium infantryman armed with spear and wooden mace. Note the decoration painted on the back of the shield. (*Photo and copyright by Julien Danielo, historical reconstruction by Letavia*)

so by a local leader called Vortigern. Little is known about Vortigern, but attempting to reconstruct this historical figure is fundamental to understanding what happened in Britannia's politics after AD 410. According to the ancient historian Gildas, who wrote the influential chronicle titled *De Excidio et Conquestu Britanniae* ('On the Ruin and Conquest of Britain'), Vortigern was a '*superbus tyrannus*', or 'proud usurper'. As we have seen, in Sub-Roman Britain the term '*tyrannus*' was used to indicate local rulers who had some political prominence but had not obtained their power with the official blessing of Rome. Before AD 410, there had already been several tyrants in Britannia, who had revolted against the Empire in an attempt to make Britain an independent nation. It is thus highly probable that Vortigern was just the last such local ruler, a warlord who had progressively brought under his control a significant portion of Britannia. After AD 410, Britain was not ruled by a single monarch, the various aristocrats with Roman origins instead beginning to administer their homelands as petty kings. The political anarchy that began in AD 410 did not last for long, as the external menaces represented by the Picts and the Scots obliged the Britons to enter some form of political unity. The territories of the various local rulers were not unified, but the numerous minor kings were probably forced to recognize the authority of an overlord who was tasked with guiding the defence of Britannia. By AD 450, Vortigern was that man.

According to Gildas, Vortigern ruled with the aid of a council that probably comprised representatives from the major *civitates* (urban centres) of Britain. These men, being aristocrats, recognized the authority of Vortigern but had their own political autonomy. Bede, another important historical source for Sub-Roman Britain, adds several details regarding Vortigern: he describes him as the man responsible for stipulating a treaty with the Saxons and provides a precise date – AD 449 – for this event. Another British chronicle, the *Historia Brittonum*, tells us that Vortigern had a son named Vortimer who helped him in ruling Britannia and was responsible for leading its military forces. This detail is particularly important, suggesting that Vortigern was in the process of creating a dynasty (differently from what the previous tyrants in Britain had done). The *Historia Brittonum* also describes the first four battles that took place between Britons and Saxons in Kent, claiming that Vortimer initially had success in fighting against the Germanic invaders. It has occasionally been suggested by modern scholars that the word 'Vortigern' could be a royal title rather than a personal name: in Brittonic language, it literally means 'Great King' or 'Overlord'. It should be noted, however, that in the Brittonic language of the Dark Ages, several names ended in 'tigern', so it is possible that what initially began as a personal name was later adopted as a term indicating a supreme ruler. Soon after having started to serve in Britain as mercenaries, the Saxon warriors invited by

Vortigern began complaining about their monthly supplies, which they considered to be inadequate. Clearly this was just a pretext for starting hostilities with the Britons, as the Germanic mercenaries – according to contemporary sources – intended to use their *foedus*/contract as just the first step towards their occupation of Britannia. Vortigern was taken by surprise by the Saxons, having previously been confident about their loyalty. Under strong pressure from the Picts, the British overlord had hoped that the Germanic leaders could secure his personal rule and save his domains from destruction. However, it soon became apparent that the Saxons were much more dangerous than the Picts and the Scots, having the ability to migrate from continental Europe to take over Britannia.

The Germanic invaders established their main base near the Kent coastline, where they could receive reinforcements and supplies from their homeland. Subsequently, Vortimer took command of the Brittonic forces and tried to limit the expansionism of the Saxons. In AD 455, in the Battle of Aylesford that took place in Kent between the Britons and the Saxons, Vortimer obtained a clear victory over the brothers Hengest and Horsa, the latter being killed. The Saxons were forced to abandon most of the territories that they had occupied in Kent, being pushed back to the coastline. At this point, however, fate intervened as Vortimer, who had almost succeeded in expelling the Germanic warriors from Britain, died, leaving the Britons without a leader. The pause in operations that followed the sudden death of Vortimer greatly favoured the Saxons, with Hengest able to reorganize his forces alongside his energetic son, Aesc. In AD 457, a further clash took place between the Britons and the Germanic invaders in Kent, with the Battle of Crecganford. This ended up in a decisive success for the Saxons, who killed 4,000 of their opponents. Following this defeat, the Britons evacuated Kent and renounced once and for all their attempt to expel the Saxons from Britannia. Having suffered such a serious defeat, they realized that the only possible option to continue the war was to limit the Saxon presence to a peripheral area of Britannia. A few years after the Battle of Crecganford, in AD 460, Hengist called for a council of all the rulers of Britain, with the promise of finding a solution to the ongoing conflict. The council, however, was a trap organized by the Saxons in order to kill the most prominent leaders of their enemies. All the Saxon warlords who attended had a knife hidden in their shoes, with which they attacked the Britons during the peace conference. In what became known as the 'Treachery of the Long Knives', dozens of Romano-Briton aristocrats were massacred and Vortigern – together with other influential leaders – was captured.

Vortigern's subsequent fate is unknown, but after AD 460 he did not take part in any recorded political event. He probably died as a captive, having been a Saxon hostage for some time. The lack of leadership that affected the Britons after the 'Treachery

Romano-Briton medium infantryman armed with spear.
(*Photo and copyright by Julien Danielo, historical reconstruction by Letavia*)

of the Long Knives' had very important consequences. In the years that followed, the Saxons began expanding their rule outside Kent and obtained a series of victories. In AD 466, the Battle of Wippedesfleot took place between the Britons and the Saxons. Despite the Germanic invaders suffered significant losses, they were able to prevail and killed twelve enemy leaders. Apparently, the clash at Wippedesfleot was the last event of a Brittonic counter-offensive that had initially achieved some success. The battle took place not far from the Saxon stronghold of Thanet, where the first groups of Germanic warriors had landed more than a decade before. This victory was obtained at a high price by Hengest and Aesc, and for some years thereafter hostilities continued at a lower intensity. By AD 465, the Saxons called their Brittonic enemies 'the Welsh', using a term that meant 'the Strangers' in their Germanic language. During the following decades, the word started to be used to indicate the Britons who resisted Saxon penetration and then the inhabitants of Wales, who were never submitted by the Anglo-Saxons. During the early AD 470s, Hengest and Aesc raided large areas of enemy territory, looting settlements and killing many civilians. Their successes encouraged more Saxons to leave continental Europe for Britannia, in search of new lands to conquer. Around AD 477, a new wave of Germanic invaders crossed the English Channel, under the leadership of the warlord Aelle and his three sons. Aelle soon proved himself a very capable military leader and – after landing in Sussex – became the new leader of the Saxons. Within

Romano-Briton medium infantryman equipped with round shield. (*Colour plate by Patricio Greve Moller, copyright of Gabriele Esposito*)

a few years, Aelle conquered the whole of Sussex, achieving an important victory over the Britons at the Battle of Mercredesburne in AD 485. Few details are known about this battle, but it is highly probable that it caused severe losses to the defeated Britons. In AD 491, Aelle besieged and conquered the important urban settlement of Andredescester (modern Pevensey), thereby securing control over the eastern portion of Sussex. As a result of these events, large swathes of eastern and central England had by 490 been permanently occupied by the Saxons. Launching devastating raids and incursions into those areas that were still free from their control, the Saxons progressively destroyed the economy of the Britons. Around AD 497, however, the politics of Britannia started to change. Aelle died (probably of natural causes), while a new capable military leader – named Ambrosius Aurelianus – emerged among the Britons. As will be seen in the next chapter, Ambrosius Aurelianus guided the resistance forces of the Britons to victory and stopped Saxon expansionism for almost an entire generation. His historical character, of which relatively little is known, later gave birth to the immortal fictional character of King Arthur.

Chapter 6

The Age of Arthur

According to Gildas, following the dramatic events of the early AD 490s, the surviving Sub-Roman aristocrats gathered together around the military leadership of Ambrosius Aurelianus, a noble from a prominent Romano-Briton family whose parents had been killed by the Saxons. Ambrosius Aurelianus soon showed himself to be both a skilled politician and a capable military leader. In a relatively short time, he was able to become the supreme leader of the Brittonic resistance and to reorganize the Sub-Roman forces. Judging from the information provided about him by Gildas, it can be said that Ambrosius Aurelianus was the 'Last of the Romans' living in Britannia. According to Gildas' text, the aristocratic family of Ambrosius Aurelianus had 'worn the purple' that was typical of Roman patricians or nobles. Senior officers of the Roman Army also 'wore the purple', so it is possible that Ambrosius Aurelianus came from an important family having a background of military leadership. Some scholars have made suggestive reconstructions about the family of Ambrosius Aurelianus, affirming that it was related to some of Britannia's latest Roman governors or even to some of Rome's imperial dynasties. Whatever the case, what is sure is that Ambrosius Aurelianus was a young but highly respected member of a Sub-Roman aristocratic family who guided the Brittonic resistance against the Saxons. Gildas, being a monk, presents Ambrosius Aurelianus as a man of exceptional virtues and obedience to God. The ancient historian wanted to use him as an example to follow for the British political leaders of his age. Ambrosius Aurelianus was surely Christian like all the Sub-Roman nobles of his time, but he was also the heir of traditional Roman military virtues. According to the *Historia Brittonum*, he belonged to a family of consular rank that had come to control a significant portion of Britannia after the evacuation of Roman troops in AD 410. The power of such a family was perceived as a threat by Vortigern, who did not want to have any rival who could challenge his position of overlord. The *Historia Brittonum* also mentions the existence of a military stronghold that was inherited by Ambrosius Aurelianus from his family. Modern historians have speculated about the existence of two rival political groups in post-AD 410 Britannia: a pro-Celtic one led by Vortigern, having as its main objective the severing of any remaining link with the Roman Empire, and a pro-Roman one led by the family of Ambrosius

Aurelianus, whose primary intention was to preserve the Roman cultural identity of Britain. When Ambrosius Aurelianus became the undisputed leader of the Britons around AD 497, the Anglo-Saxon invaders already securely controlled several areas of England: the Isle of Wight, Kent, Lincolnshire, Norfolk and Suffolk, as well as some coastal portions of Northumberland and Yorkshire. The conflict with the Germanic invaders had depopulated many towns and cities, including Londinium (modern London), which had been almost abandoned by its inhabitants.

Ambrosius Aurelianus revived the remnants of the Roman provincial administration and reorganized the Brittonic military forces, probably by using former *limitanei* troops as their core. For several years he fought with great success against the Saxons, using hit-and-run and scorched earth tactics, as a result of which he was able to slow down the Saxon occupation of western England. Counting on the support of the warlike Welsh communities, who had started to be threatened by the Saxons, Ambrosius Aurelianus was later able to gather a larger army and fight on the open field against the Germanic invaders at the famous Battle of Badon Hill. Very little is known about the composition of Ambrosius Aurelianus' forces, but it is sure that over time they started to include a number of heavily armoured cavalry. These, being equipped in Late Roman fashion, became elite shock troops that – thanks to their higher degree of mobility – could attack the Saxons whenever they wanted and without running the risk of being intercepted. The Saxons had only small numbers of horsemen at their disposal, their armies mostly consisting of infantry. Under the leadership of Ambrosius Aurelianus, the Britons experienced a degree of unity that had not been seen for decades, which was one of the key factors behind their unexpected success.

Around the year AD 500, a major and decisive clash took place between the Britons and the Saxons, which is commonly known as the Battle of Badon Hill (*Mons Badonicus* in Latin), which is thought to have taken place in Wiltshire. No exact date is known for the clash, nor is it known if it was a pitched battle or a siege (as suggested by Gildas). It probably consisted of a Briton attack directed against a Saxon fortified position located on top of a hill. According to various sources it lasted for more than one day, with Ambrosius Aurelianus bearing the sign of the Christian cross on his shield (like Emperor Constantine had done at the Battle of the Milvian Bridge several decades before). It is highly probable that the heavy cavalry of Ambrosius Aurelianus played a prominent role at Badon Hill and that they caused heavy losses to the Saxons, whom they crushed. The Battle of Badon Hill was a great victory for Ambrosius Aurelianus and his Britons. Thereafter, the Saxons temporarily halted their occupation of western England for almost a generation. The ancient sources do not mention Ambrosius Aurelianus in describing the events that followed the clash, so it is likely that the Romano-Briton leader died soon after the battle.

Romano-Briton light infantryman armed with spear and throwing javelins. (*Photo and copyright by Julien Danielo, historical reconstruction by Letavia*)

Romano-Briton light infantryman armed with spear, heavy javelin and sword. (*Colour plate by Patricio Greve Moller, copyright of Gabriele Esposito*)

Following the death of their great warlord, the Britons were no longer able to face the Saxons on equal terms, their political fragmentation becoming an increasingly serious problem. By AD 520, the Saxons controlled Kent, Sussex, East Anglia, Hampshire and Yorkshire. They started organizing their possessions as small autonomous kingdoms while continuing to fight against the Britons in order to expand their territories. In AD 535 and AD 536, the whole of Britain experienced extreme weather events that caused a great famine. This seriously affected western England and Wales – which were still under control of the Britons – and was followed by a great plague in AD 549. The Saxons took advantage of their enemies' difficulties to continue their conquest of England, gaining more victories in clashes such as the Battle of Beran Byrig (AD 556) and the Battle of Bedcanford (AD 571). These encounters took place near important fortifications of the Britons, which are now commonly known as hill forts. The latter were similar to the pre-Roman *oppida* fortifications of the Celts. Apparently, Ambrosius Aurelianus had built a network of such forts across Britannia to work as operational bases for his fast-moving cavalry. Thanks to their victory at Bedcanford, the Saxons occupied four hill forts: Limbury, Avlesbury, Benson and Eynsham. The successes of the invaders, however, did not prevent the Britons from fighting against each other during some small-scale civil wars, the political unity achieved under Ambrosius Aurelianus having been completely lost due to the personal ambitions of the various Sub-Roman petty kings. In AD 577, the Saxons obtained another great victory at the Battle of Dyrham, thanks to which they could complete their conquest of Wessex. The Brittonic settlements of present-day Gloucester, Cirencester and Bath were all taken by the Saxons. This clash marked a real turning point in the long war fought between the Britons and the Saxons, enabling the Germanic invaders to overrun the salient still controlled by the Britons around the London area and to annex the Midlands. With the occupation of Watling Street and Bath, the Saxons could finally separate the Britons living in Wales from those who were still free in south-western England. Following these events, the Britons' defences in the English Midlands collapsed and the Saxons overran the enemy defensive line running along Watling Street, the most important road built in Britain by the Romans, which ran from the Kent coast in the east to the border of Wales in the west, passing through Londinium. By breaking the British salient – which had probably been established by Ambrosius Aurelianus after the Battle of Badon Hill – the Saxons united the areas of England that were under their control and conquered the Midlands. The border dividing the Britons of Wales from the Saxons was established at the Wansdyke along the ridge of the Mendip Hills. The Saxon victory at the Battle of Fethanleag in AD 584 then broke forever any hope of Brittonic resistance in the heart of England.

During the second half of the sixth century, the Angles and Jutes were also particularly active in settling more lands taken from the Britons. The Angles moved

Romano-Briton archer wearing a *pileus pannonicus* cap made of fur. (*Colour plate by Patricio Greve Moller, copyright of Gabriele Esposito*)

Romano-Briton archer. (*Photo and copyright by Julien Danielo, historical reconstruction by Letavia*)

north along the coastline of eastern England, while the Jutes became predominant in Kent. In AD 590, several kings of the Britons formed a military alliance in the hope of stopping the Saxons in Wiltshire, like Ambrosius Aurelianus had done almost a century before. Against all odds, they defeated the Saxons at the Battle of Woden's Burg in AD 592, thereby gaining time to reorganize their defences. The new Brittonic alliance was led by Urien of Rheged, a monarch who ruled a small Sub-Roman kingdom in north-western England just south of Hadrian's Wall. While these events took place in the west, in the east the Angles continued their expansion across Northumbria and – in AD 596 – landed a large invading force on the Fife coast in south-eastern Scotland. The Picts and the Scots, who had long been at war with the Britons, realized that the Germanic warriors also represented a deadly menace for them, and thus joined forces with the Britons in a temporary military alliance. However, they were soon defeated by the Angles at the Battle of Raith. Following this clash, the Britons' presence in north-eastern England was seriously weakened and the alliance between the Picts and the Scots came to an abrupt end. Shortly after these events, Urien of Rheged was murdered and the alliance of Brittonic kings that he had created crumbled. Two rival factions subsequently emerged among the Britons and a new civil war broke out. In AD 597, Pope Gregory I sent St Augustin of Canterbury to Kent with orders to convert to Christianity the Germani living in Britain. This had a significant symbolic importance, since it showed to the Britons that even the papacy in Rome no longer had any trust in their possibility to resist.

By AD 600, most of the territory of present-day England had been conquered by the Saxons, Angles and Jutes, with only some small areas of north-western England remaining independent of their rule. The Angles progressively extended their dominance over East Anglia, Mercia and Northumbria, defeating the Britons first at the Battle of Catraeth and then at the Battle of Chester. The latter clash, taking place in AD 616, was of particular importance as it severed the last land connection existing between Wales and the Brittonic communities that were still resisting in north-western England. In 633, at the Battle of Hatfield Chase, the Britons of Wales defeated the Angles of Northumbria after having formed a temporary alliance with the Saxons of Mercia. During the following year, however, the Welsh were expelled from Northumbria after the Battle of Heayenfield. Despite this setback, the alliance between Britons of Wales and Saxons of Mercia continued to hold. In AD 644, the Angles were defeated at the Battle of Maserfield, but in AD 655 the destiny of northern England was finally decided at the Battle of the Winwaed, which saw the definitive defeat of the Mercians – led by their king, Penda – and their Welsh allies. By 658, the Welsh had been driven back as far as the Parrett River in Somerset, the Angles by then dominating northern England. While these events took place in the north, the Jutes – in the south – also established themselves on the Isle of Wight and in some areas of Hampshire. From a military point of view, the Saxons were much stronger than the Angles and the Jutes, being more numerous and warlike. The co-existence between Germanic invaders and Brittonic communities along the new Welsh frontier was a difficult one for most of the eighth century. The first half of this period saw several

Romano-Briton warrior armed with a Late Roman prototype of a crossbow.
(*Photo and copyright by Julien Danielo, historical reconstruction by Letavia*)

clashes taking place between the Welsh petty kingdoms and the new Germanic states that were emerging in England. These culminated with the Battle of Hereford in AD 760, which ended with a decisive victory for the Saxons of Mercia over their Welsh enemies. The Saxon conquest of England had been a very long and difficult one, due to the strong resistance of the Britons; it had lasted almost two centuries and had caused terrible devastation of British lands. Militarily, it can be divided into two main phases: AD 449–500 and 500–660. The first phase, ending with the victory of Ambrosius Aurelianus at the Battle of Badon Hill, probably culminated with the signing of a peace treaty between the Britons and the Saxons that remained in place for a number of years. According to archaeological finds, a border was created between the Briton lands and those of the Saxon around AD 500; this stretched from York in the north to Bournemouth in the south and divided England into two parts. The western portion, united with Wales, remained independent from the Germanic invaders, while the eastern one was settled quite rapidly by the Saxons. The period AD 500–660 was characterized by a series of defeats for the resisting Britons and the final victory of the Saxons.

Romano-Briton heavy cavalryman wearing a helmet decorated with painted gems. (*Colour plate by Patricio Greve Moller, copyright of Gabriele Esposito*)

Chapter 7

The Saxon Heptarchy

Following the fall of western and southern England, many Britons migrated to Armorica in north-western Gaul, a region inhabited by Romano-Celtic communities that had a lot in common with those of Sub-Roman Britain. As a result of this migration, Armorica started to be known as 'Brittany' and became a sanctuary for political refugees from the former Britannia (including Gildas, whose work *De Excidio et Conquestu Britanniae* is our main primary source for reconstructing the Saxon conquest of England). Despite the final victory of the Saxons, the culture of Sub-Roman Britain continued to survive – albeit in a different version – after 660. Between north-western England and south-western Scotland, various Briton realms collectively known as the 'Old North' emerged: Ebrauc, Bryneich, Rheged, Elmet, Gododdin and Strathclyde. The latter, in particular, became quite powerful and continued to exist as an autonomous political entity until AD 945. Its capital, Dumbarton, was known as the 'Rock of the Britons' in the Early Middle Ages. The Briton communities living in Wales and Cornwall also remained independent from the Saxons after AD 660, the harsh nature of their homelands enabling them to repulse several aggressive invasions. Cornwall was finally submitted by the Saxons only during the reign of Alfred the Great, while the small Briton princedoms in Wales were never conquered by the Saxons. The Welsh conducted a low-intensity guerrilla war against the Saxons and were able to achieve a series of local victories over many decades. Consequently, together with the Old North, Wales remained the home of Sub-Roman Britain culture for many years. During the whole period AD 410–660 the Picts and Scots played a crucial role in the history of Britain. For example, as we have seen, their expansionism was the main cause behind the Britons' decision to invite the Saxons onto their lands. Initially, the Picts and Scots fought against each other, the Scots occupying a large part of Scotland's western coastline (in modern Argyll) that had previously been inhabited by the Picts. By AD 600, the Scots living in Argyll had created the Kingdom of Dál Riata, a powerful political entity that continued to exist until AD 730. Following St Patrick's evangelization of Ireland, the Scots of Britain converted to Christianity too. Having a sizeable fleet of warships, they dominated the Irish Sea for a long time. The Picts controlled most of Scotland for the whole period AD 410–660, and on several occasions allied themselves with the

Romano-Briton heavy cavalryman equipped with scale armour and metal greaves. (*Photo and copyright by Julien Danielo, historical reconstruction by Letavia*)

Romano-Briton heavy cavalryman. The decorative patterns of his clothing show a clear Celtic influence. (*Colour plate by Patricio Greve Moller, copyright of Gabriele Esposito*)

Scots to attack the Britons. Around AD 730, however, the Picts finally conquered the Kingdom of Dál Riata after a series of hard-fought campaigns and thus absorbed the Scots of Britain.

Since AD 660, following the end of the 'conquest era', the new Germanic inhabitants of England started to establish their recently acquired possessions as proper kingdoms. These soon began to fight against each other for dominance over England, with seven states eventually emerging from the conflicts that ravaged southern Britain. This new political system, known as the 'Heptarchy' due to the number of kingdoms that formed it, was relatively stable and continued to exist until the arrival of the Vikings decisively altered the balance of power in England. The seven kingdoms that made up the Heptarchy were: Wessex, Essex, Sussex, Mercia, East Anglia, Northumbria and Kent. The first four were inhabited by the Saxons, with East Anglia and Northumbria settled by the Angles and Kent containing the Jutes. However, until the ascendancy of Alfred the Great, the states comprising the Heptarchy were not the only ones existing in England, as several sub-kingdoms were formed over time. These were usually client states of the major realms, but sometimes – for short periods of time – they acted as autonomous political entities. According to Germanic traditions, a kingdom was part of a monarch's private properties, so when a king died, his territorial possessions were usually divided between his sons, meaning the unity of a realm could easily be destroyed. On several occasions, the political fragmentation that usually followed successions caused the outbreak of civil wars, the heirs of the dead monarch fighting against each other in a bid to recreate a unified state under the leadership of the strongest rival. Political competition was extremely strong between the kingdoms of the Heptarchy, with possession of some geographical areas – such as the Kingdom of Middlesex, which soon became known as Mercia – being hotly contested. Differently from what happened in other areas of Europe – like France or Spain – where the Germanic peoples organized their newly conquered lands as large and unified kingdoms, in England they structured their territorial possessions as minor realms of a tribal nature.

The Kingdom of Kent, the only realm of the Jutes in England, was the first state of the Heptarchy to disappear. The Jutes, while less numerous than the Saxons, controlled an area of England that had great strategic importance. In AD 676, the Kingdom of Kent was attacked by Mercia; the ensuing conflict, according to contemporary sources, was extremely violent, with the Saxons devastating the Jutes' lands and desecrating many churches and monasteries. Life in the Kingdom of Kent was characterized by a pacific co-existence between the local Briton population and the Jutes, with a substantial number of Jutes having converted to Christianity. The Mercian invasion put an end to this situation and caused great losses to the population of Kent. In AD 681, the Saxons of Mercia mounted a fresh invasion of Jute lands, advancing deeply into southern Hampshire and conquering the Isle of Wight. The island, which had been an important naval base of the Jutes for many years, was given by the Mercians to the Kingdom of Sussex, which was their main military ally. The Kingdom of Kent was the most culturally advanced realm in England, its rulers issuing laws that were influenced by Roman legal traditions and respected the way of life of their Briton subjects. In AD 685, however, the realm was ravaged by a civil war that saw the involvement of Sussex. Although the conflict did not last long, it caused further damage to the Jutes of southern England. During the late seventh century Caedwalla, King of Wessex, decided to eliminate the Jutes' presence in south-eastern England, having become concerned that Mercia or Sussex could permanently occupy Kent. As a result, after a brief period of fighting, Caedwalla conquered the Jutes' remaining lands in Hampshire and their former lands in Kent that had temporarily been occupied by Sussex. The Isle of Wight was also annexed to Wessex. By AD 700, the Jutes of southern England were no longer independent: their communities in Hampshire and on the Isle of Wight were absorbed into the Kingdom of Wessex, while Kent was transformed into a semi-autonomous puppet state dominated by the West Saxons.

Mercia, the last of the Heptarchy's kingdoms to convert to Christianity, started its development as an autonomous realm around AD 584. It was inhabited by the warlike tribal groups of the Middle Saxons, who gradually came to control the following areas of central England: Derbyshire, Leicestershire, Nottinghamshire, Northamptonshire, Staffordshire and Warwickshire. During the early seventh century, Mercia fought on several occasions against Northumbria, whose leaders wanted to expand their realm southwards. In AD 655, at the Battle of the Winwaed, the Mercians were defeated by the Northumbrians, leading to a period of Northumbrian dominance over the Middle Saxons. However, this did not last for long since, the Mercians revolting against the northern invaders in AD 658 and re-establishing an independent Kingdom of Mercia. In AD 679, at the Battle of the Trent, the Mercians secured a great victory over Northumbria, thanks to which the Middle Saxons were able to settle once and for all the long-disputed border that separated their lands from those of the Angles. Between AD 716 and AD 757, the Kingdom of Mercia was ruled by a very capable monarch named Aethelbald, who was able to establish Mercia's hegemony over most of the Anglo-Saxon lands located south of the Humber and spent most of his life fighting against Wessex. In AD 752, the West Saxons defeated Aethelbald in battle, but he recovered very rapidly and was soon able to restore his influence over a large portion of England. Following the death of Aethelbald, who was assassinated by one of his bodyguards, an extremely violent civil war broke out

Romano-Briton heavy cavalryman carrying a windsock standard of the draco type. (*Colour plate by Patricio Greve Moller, copyright of Gabriele Esposito*)

Romano-Briton warrior carrying a windsock draco standard. These were invented by the Sarmatians and then adopted by the Late Roman Army. (*Photo and copyright by Julien Danielo, historical reconstruction by Letavia*)

within Mercia, which ended with the ascendancy of Offa as ruler of the Middle Saxons. Offa renewed the expansionist policy of his predecessor and became the greatest monarch in the history of Mercia. He secured control of most of southern England through a series of campaigns. Offa also greatly improved the standard of living of his subjects, reforming the administrative structures of his realm and overseeing the first major issues of gold coins in Anglo-Saxon England. Offa was so capable and well-known a monarch that he even negotiated with the great Holy Roman Emperor, Charlemagne, as an equal. Under his rule, Mercia was the leading power of southern Britain and one of the most important Germanic states in Europe. Offa also favoured the spreading of Christianity in his domains, which had very significant cultural consequences. The great monarch died in AD 796, being succeeded by a series of kings who failed to live up to his high standards. By the beginning of the new century, the ascendancy of Wessex under the leadership of Egbert caused a gradual decline of Mercia's military power. In AD 825, at the Battle of Ellandun, the Mercians were defeated by the West Saxons, after which Egbert came to dominate Mercia. In AD 830, after a short period of domination by Wessex, the Middle Saxons revolted and regained their independence. Nevertheless, their kingdom had ceased to be the dominant power of Anglo-Saxon England and would soon be threatened by the arrival of the Vikings.

Essex emerged as a unified kingdom during the late sixth century, its population adopting the Christian faith during the early years of the seventh century. Initially, the East Saxons were under the political influence of the Kingdom of Kent, but they gradually became the more powerful realm. The Christianization of Essex was a very complex process, the Germanic communities of the kingdom never fully accepting the new faith. Consequently, for almost a century, the monarchs of Essex had different religious positions: some of them were favourable to the new faith, whereas others temporarily restored their pagan traditions. After Christianity became well-established in the realm, the East Saxons experienced some years of military expansion, but they were never able to become a major power of the Heptarchy. The ascendancy of Wessex and Mercia had long-lasting consequences politically for Essex, which was forced to give up most of its earlier conquests. By AD 750, the Mercians had transformed Essex into one of their vassals, but the East Saxons continued to have a degree of autonomy. Following the defeat of Mercian monarch Beornwulf in AD 825 by the West Saxons, the Kingdom of Essex ceased to be a tributary state of Mercia and was absorbed into the Kingdom of Wessex. Before the arrival of the Vikings, Essex was for some decades part of a sub-realm dominated by Wessex that also comprised Kent.

Detail of the spangenhelm helmet worn by a Romano-Briton warrior.
(Photo and copyright by Julien Danielo, historical reconstruction by Letavia)

Detail of the spangenhelm helmet worn by a Romano-Briton warrior.
(*Photo and copyright by Julien Danielo, historical reconstruction by Letavia*)

Sussex assumed the form of a unified kingdom only around AD 607, after its tribal communities fought a bloody war against the West Saxons. In order to retain their independence, the South Saxons formed a strong military alliance with the Mercians and fought with them against Wessex. Due to the contribution it had made in the conflict against the West Saxons, Sussex received the Isle of Wight from Mercia. The island was mostly populated by Jutes, and it was not easy for the South Saxons to colonize it effectively. In AD 681, most of Sussex's population was baptized; a few years later, the kingdom attacked Kent and occupied most of its territory. This proved a 'golden age' for the South Saxons, but it was not to last for long. Wessex soon decided to take advantage of Kent's fall by occupying most of the Jutes' territories that had been recently conquered by the South Saxons. Caedwalla, ruler of Wessex, later also invaded Sussex and briefly transformed it into a puppet state. The West Saxons occupied the Isle of Wight and ruthlessly massacred its Jute population. For several decades, the Kingdom of Sussex was a vassal of Wessex, joining in a campaign against the Britons living in Cornwall. Following the outbreak of a civil war in Wessex, the South Saxons were able to regain their full independence in AD 722. The Kingdom of Wessex launched at least three campaigns against Sussex during subsequent years, but the South Saxons were able to retain their recently regained freedom. The ascendancy of Mercia under Offa later became a serious menace to Sussex's independence, especially after the Mercians established their control over Kent. By AD 772, after just a few months of campaigning, Offa had been able to occupy the whole of Sussex and annexed it to Mercia. Following Offa's death, Mercia rapidly ceased to be a major military power, meaning the South Saxons were able to regain their autonomy. Yet this proved only quite short-lived, as after the Battle of Ellandun in AD 825 the Kingdom of Sussex was transformed into a vassal state of Wessex. Organized as a semi-autonomous earldom, the territory of the South Saxons was united with that of Kent before being merged with the other lands of the West Saxons.

The West Saxons, living on territory that bordered with the lands of the Britons, played a very important role during the campaigns that saw the ascendancy of the Saxons in south-western England. They fought with great determination against the Sub-Roman communities facing them and – despite suffering some temporary setbacks – were finally able to secure their control over a vast area of England. The Kingdom of Wessex was one of the last Anglo-Saxon realms to develop as a unified political entity, as during the 'age of conquest' the warlike West Saxons continued to live according to their tribal traditions. By AD 630, however, a unified state had emerged, one that soon adopted Christianity as its new faith, after Cynegils (one of the West Saxons' early kings) was baptized in AD 640. An episcopal see was established at Dorchester, which rapidly became the most important urban centre of early Wessex. During the mid-seventh century, the West Saxons came under increasing pressure from Mercia, which was expanding very rapidly and had become the dominant military power of Anglo-Saxon England. Mercian attacks deprived Wessex of lands north of the River Thames and caused serious losses to the West Saxons. Despite being frequently at war with the Mercians, the Kingdom of Wessex launched a series of effective campaigns against the Britons still living in south-western England and continued to flourish from a cultural point of view. A second episcopal see, for example, was established during this period at Winchester. One of the most capable kings of the West Saxons during the late seventh century was Caedwalla, who reigned only for a brief period but was able to achieve a notable expansion of his kingdom, swiftly conquering Kent and Sussex, together with the Isle of Wight. Ine, Caedwalla's successor, reigned for a long period (thirty-eight years) and issued an important code of laws. The early eighth century was an extremely difficult time for the Kingdom of Wessex, which was overshadowed by the expanding Kingdom of Mercia. Wessex was the only state of southern Britain that was not transformed into a client realm of the Mercians. Despite suffering some military defeats, it continued to grow from economically and was even able to complete the conquest of the last Briton strongholds in Dumnonia (Devon). The territories contested by Mercia and Wessex – Gloucestershire and Oxfordshire – were extremely rich. The heartland of the West Saxons, however, consisted of Hampshire, Wiltshire, Berkshire, Dorset and Somerset.

Differently from the Jutes, the Angles remained mostly independent from the Saxons, their two kingdoms of East Anglia and Northumbria flourishing for many years. East Anglia was established as a realm during the second half of the sixth century but soon started to come under the influence of Mercia when the latter began expanding. Initially, the East Angles were a strong military power, defeating the monarch of Northumbria – Aethelfrith – in AD 616 and replacing him with a new king who was more favourable towards them (the future Edwin of Northumbria). However, the Angles of Northumbria soon regained their autonomy from those of East Anglia and their realm became increasingly powerful. In AD 604, Raedwald, king of the East Anglians, was baptized, but his kingdom continued to see the co-existence of pagan rituals with the new Christian ones. The military skill of Raedwald made him the most important king in the history of East Anglia. By protecting the young Edwin, an exiled noble from Northumbria, he became an enemy of King Aethelfrith. Edwin was a claimant to the Northumbrian throne and an extremely dangerous rival for Aethelfrith, who had obtained power through the support of his warriors. Initially, Aethelfrith sent messengers to Raedwald offering a large sum of

Saxon warrior wearing a helmet with facial mask. (*Photo by Viveka Sjölund, copyright by Uttaharjar*)

Saxon warrior armed with spear, sword and axe. (*Photo and copyright by Lindsay Kerr of Wulfheodenas*)

money in return for Edwin's death. Raedwald refused to comply, having established a very positive relationship with Edwin and considering him the only legitimate King of Northumbria. Aethelfrith repeated his offers for a second and for a third time, but Raedwald responded by waging war on Northumbria in order to place Edwin on the throne. In late AD 616, the monarch of East Anglia assembled an army and marched north, along the coast of eastern England, with the objective of defeating the Northumbrians. The opposing forces met on the east bank of the Idle River, where a fierce clash took place. According to ancient sources, the two armies of Angles fought with great violence, to the point that the Idle River 'was fould with blood'. At the end of the battle, both Aethelfrith and Raedwald's son, Raegenhere, were dead. Edwin could thus succeed Aethelfrith as King of Northumbria but was also chosen as Raedwald's successor for the Kingdom of East Anglia. After winning the Battle of the Idle, Raedwald became the most powerful and respected monarch of the Heptarchy. Due to his indirect dominance over Northumbria, he became known as *Rex Anglorum*, or 'King of the Angles'.

Around AD 640, the Kingdom of East Anglia was attacked for the first time on a large scale by the Mercians, who obtained a series of victories over the Angles. Following the Battle of Bulcamp, which took place in AD 654, the Kingdom of East Anglia was transformed into a vassal state of Mercia. The hegemony of the Middle Saxons over the East Angles lasted for more than a century, until Offa of Mercia annexed East Anglia to his domains in AD 794. Following Offa's death, there was a brief revival of East Anglian independence, with the Angles revolting against their Saxon overlords. But the rebellion was crushed quite easily by the Mercians, after which thus another period of Saxon control over East Anglia began. In AD 825, the East Anglians revolted again against Mercia under the leadership of Aethelstan. This time the rebellion ended with victory for the Angles, who defeated and killed two Mercian kings. By AD 827, with the collapse of Mercia's military power, the Kingdom of East Anglia was again a fully independent state. The East Angles formed a strong alliance with Wessex and acknowledged Egbert (monarch of the West Saxons) as their overlord. Nonetheless, East Anglia remained fully autonomous from any other kingdom of the Heptarchy until the arrival of the Vikings.

The Angles who settled on the north-eastern coast of England initially organized their newly conquered territories as two autonomous political entities, known as Bernicia and Deira. These frequently fought against each other until being unified into a single kingdom around AD 654. Deira controlled most of Yorkshire, while Bernicia comprised most of the other lands that later became part of Northumbria. The Angles of the north did not have a very positive relationship with those who had already settled in East Anglia, with several conflicts taking place between

Northumbria and the East Angles during the seventh century. In AD 616, a pretender to the Northumbrian throne, named Edwin, formed an alliance with Raedwald of East Anglia and later temporarily ruled both realms of the Angles. In the long run, however, it became apparent that the Northumbrians would remain independent and that – over time – they would become more powerful than East Anglia. For most of its early history, the Kingdom of Northumbria was greatly damaged by the frequent dynastic struggles that broke out between its aristocratic groups. The former royal families of Bernicia and Deira fought each other on several occasions in order to determine which of them would rule a unified Northumbria. The realm, compared with the other states of the Heptarchy, always retained a distinct tribal nature. Its warriors were famed for their courage and combat skill, mostly because they spent their lives fighting against the peoples of Scotland. One of Northumbria's greatest monarchs was Edwin, who ruled from AD 616–633. He occupied the Isle of Man and exerted his influence over much of northern Wales before converting to the Christian faith in AD 627. In AD 633, Edwin of Northumbria was defeated in battle by an alliance comprising the Welsh princedom of Gwynedd and the Saxon Kingdom of Mercia. Edwin's successor, Oswald, tried to preserve the internal unity of Northumbria and built the famous monastery of Lindisfarne, but was defeated and killed by the Mercians at the Battle of Maserfield in AD 642. Oswiu, brother and successor of Oswald, avenged him by defeating the Mercians at the Battle of the Winwaed. Oswiu was a very capable king and a key figure behind the process that led to the Christianization of northern England. The Northumbrians gradually started to exert a strong influence over the Picts, defeating them in AD 671 and assuming control over the lands located between the Firth of Forth and the River Tweed. During the following years, the Northumbrians were frequently at war with Mercia, mostly for dominance over the Kingdom of Lindsey (a sub-realm of Mercia). The campaigns conducted against the Middle Saxons, however, were not particularly successful, and in AD 685 a Northumbrian invasion of Pictish lands ended in complete failure. Following the Picts' decisive victory at the Battle of Dun Nechtain, Northumbria entered a long period of slow decline. The realm lost its prominence over the Kingdom of Lindsey and started to suffer from incursions by the Picts. A long border was established between Mercia and Northumbria, which ran across most of England from the River Humber in the east to the River Mersey in the west. This frontier line was well defended on both sides, being fortified with massive earthworks. During the late seventh century, Bernicia and Deira continued to be ruled as autonomous parts of the same kingdom, which gradually regained part of its previous importance by establishing some sort of control over the eastern Lowlands of Scotland.

Saxon warlord equipped with the panoply discovered at Sutton Hoo.
(*Colour plate by Patricio Greve Moller, copyright of Gabriele Esposito*)

Saxon warrior bearing a standard. (*Photo and copyright by Lindsay Kerr of Wulfheodenas*)

Chapter 8

Sub-Roman Military Organization and Weapons

The Sub-Roman military forces of the Britons partly inherited the general organization that had been introduced in the Roman Army by Emperor Constantine. In the early decades of the fourth century AD, Constantine carried on a major military reform which was based on the separation of the field troops from those on the border. The field troops were to be garrisoned in the major cities of the Empire, as highly mobile strategic reserves, while the border troops were based along the frontiers of the Empire in order to serve as the first line of defence against foreign attacks. As we have seen, all units of the Roman Army were now divided into two large categories: the *comitatenses* (field troops) and the *limitanei* (border troops). After the Romans evacuated Britain in AD 410, the *comitatenses* went to continental Europe, whereas most of the more lightly armed *limitanei* remained behind, where they soon became the core of the new Sub-Roman units. As a consequence, the armies of the Britons that opposed the Germanic invasion of England still looked very similar to the Roman troops of the time. This was not strictly true for the Britons of Wales, whose contingents were usually recruited and organized along tribal lines according to old Celtic traditions. The Welsh warriors, in particular, were renowned light infantry skirmishers, equipped with throwing javelins and bows which made them masters in organizing effective ambushes and conducting hit-and-run operations like their pre-Roman ancestors.

The new Sub-Roman troops, especially regarding their equipment, appeared much the same as the Late Roman soldiers who had garrisoned their island during the previous decades. The military fashions of Sub-Roman Britain were almost identical to those of the Late Roman Empire. Most of the Sub-Roman foot soldiers did not wear armour, being equipped with just a helmet. Over time, the numbers of Sub-Roman light infantry expanded significantly. The heavy cavalry, considered the elite of the Sub-Roman military, was mostly recruited from the wealthiest members of society. Thanks to their high-quality and effective personal equipment, the heavy cavalrymen played a decisive role on the battlefields of Britannia. The forces opposing the Anglo-Saxon invasion of England were equipped with a mix of Sub-Roman and Celtic elements. The standard armour of the Brittonic heavy foot soldiers was the *lorica hamata*, or chainmail, which varied in size, for example being

Saxon warrior armed with sword and seax short sword. (*Photo and copyright by Lindsay Kerr of Wulfheodenas*)

Saxon warrior wearing a helmet with facial mask. (*Photo by Viveka Sjölund, copyright by Uttaharjar*)

either long- or short-sleeved. This was worn in combination with a helmet of Late Roman design, which – in most cases – belonged to the extensive family of ridge helmets. The Britons attacked the invading Anglo-Saxons by employing effective hit-and-run tactics, their foot troops mostly consisting of fast-moving skirmishers who could operate on any kind of terrain. During the Late Roman period, archery was practiced on a significant scale in Britannia, the locally recruited Roman forces including several units of bowmen. Archery became increasingly important in Wales after the Anglo-Saxons occupied most of England, the Welsh warriors significantly improving their wooden longbows and transforming them into very effective missile weapons.

During the Crisis of the Third Century, the general appearance of Roman soldiers became quite different from that reproduced on Trajan's Column: the traditional image of the legionaries equipped with segmented armour and the auxiliaries with chainmail was no longer in existence by AD 284. The Crisis of the Third Century saw a progressive collapse of Rome's central administration, which had important consequences for the organization of the military but also for the supply system that had previously functioned so well. During those years of anarchy, regular soldiers started to receive new clothing and weapons on a much more irregular basis, resulting in a reduction of the earlier high level of standardization. Diocletian and Constantine did what was possible to rebuild the supply system of the army: by the beginning of the fifth century AD there were thirty-five state *fabricae* (factories) located across the Empire and producing materials for the armed forces. Each state factory was under the control of a Procurator and protected by a small garrison. The expenses for production of military materials were still paid by the central administration, thanks to the existence of a specific tax. After the definitive division of the Empire in AD 395, however, different levels of uniformity became apparent between the units of the Western Empire and those of the Eastern Empire. Tax revenues of the eastern regions were almost double those in the West, with the result that soldiers from Gaul or Italy started to be equipped with materials of inferior quality. Generally speaking, the clothing and equipment of the *comitatenses* showed a higher degree of uniformity than those of the *limitanei*, who mostly bought their clothing from small local stores attached to their frontier forts. As had been the case for the auxilia of previous centuries, the weapons and equipment of the *limitanei* were strongly influenced by the military fashions of the peoples living along the Roman frontiers (both inside and outside the Empire).

During the Middle Empire, the main garment worn by Roman soldiers was still the tunic, although this had greatly changed since the times of Augustus. The Arch of Severus, which was completed at the very beginning of the third century AD, still shows Roman soldiers with the traditional kind of tunic worn during the Early Empire. The following years of crisis, however, changed this, the central decades of the third century seeing the widespread introduction of the new long-sleeved tunic. This was copied from the contemporary dress of Germanic warriors, who had worn it on a large scale for a long time. The Roman terminology for this garment was *tunica manicata*, which was generally made of wool during the winter and linen in the summer. The *tunica manicata* was basically a simple T-shaped garment, with tight sleeves and usually reaching to the knees. It was not made of cut-and-sewn parts, but woven entire in a single piece: it was folded in half and sewn up the sides, with a neck slit cut in the centre. The *tunica manicata* was generally decorated with woven or attached strips and circular roundels of cloth, known respectively *clavi* and *orbiculi*. Both these decorative elements usually comprised geometrical patterns and stylized plant motifs, but could also include human or animal figures. The *clavi* were narrow vertical bands of cloth running from the top to the bottom of the tunic, while the *orbiculi* were patterned roundels on the shoulders and skirt of the tunic. The standard colours for military tunics were red and white, the latter being extremely popular in the hottest eastern regions. After the tunic, the cloak remained the second most important garment of the Roman soldier; hip-length and semi-circular, it was known as a *sagum*. It could be decorated with fringes or with applied decorations of the same kind worn on tunic. The cloaks of officers were different from those of the soldiers, being longer (ankle-length) and trapezoid in shape. They were not decorated with *clavi* or *orbiculi*, but instead had large embroidered panels in the form of a square, known as *tabula*. All cloaks were pinned up on the right shoulder by a large brooch, which could be richly decorated if worn by a senior officer. Materials and colours were more or less the same as for the tunics, with wool for winter and linen for summer, red and white being the most popular colours.

During the late third century AD, Roman military belts started to show a strong Germanic influence, especially in the decorations. Bronze or iron fittings became increasingly popular, both cast and chiselled, being embellished with punched or carved work. By the time of Diocletian and Constantine, most of the soldiers wore *bracae*, or trousers. Regarding footwear, the traditional model of open sandals known as *caligae* had completely disappeared by the end of the third century, being replaced by new front-fastening short boots with integrally cut laces. As for headgear, when not wearing a helmet, soldiers on active service usually had a particular kind of cap known as a *pileus pannonicus*. This could be made from felt or napped wool, and could be smooth or shaggy, low or tall. The cylindrical shape made this kind of cap very comfortable and easy to produce: apparently it started to be used during the early third century, also being adopted as a sign of distinction by civilian dignitaries. This pillbox

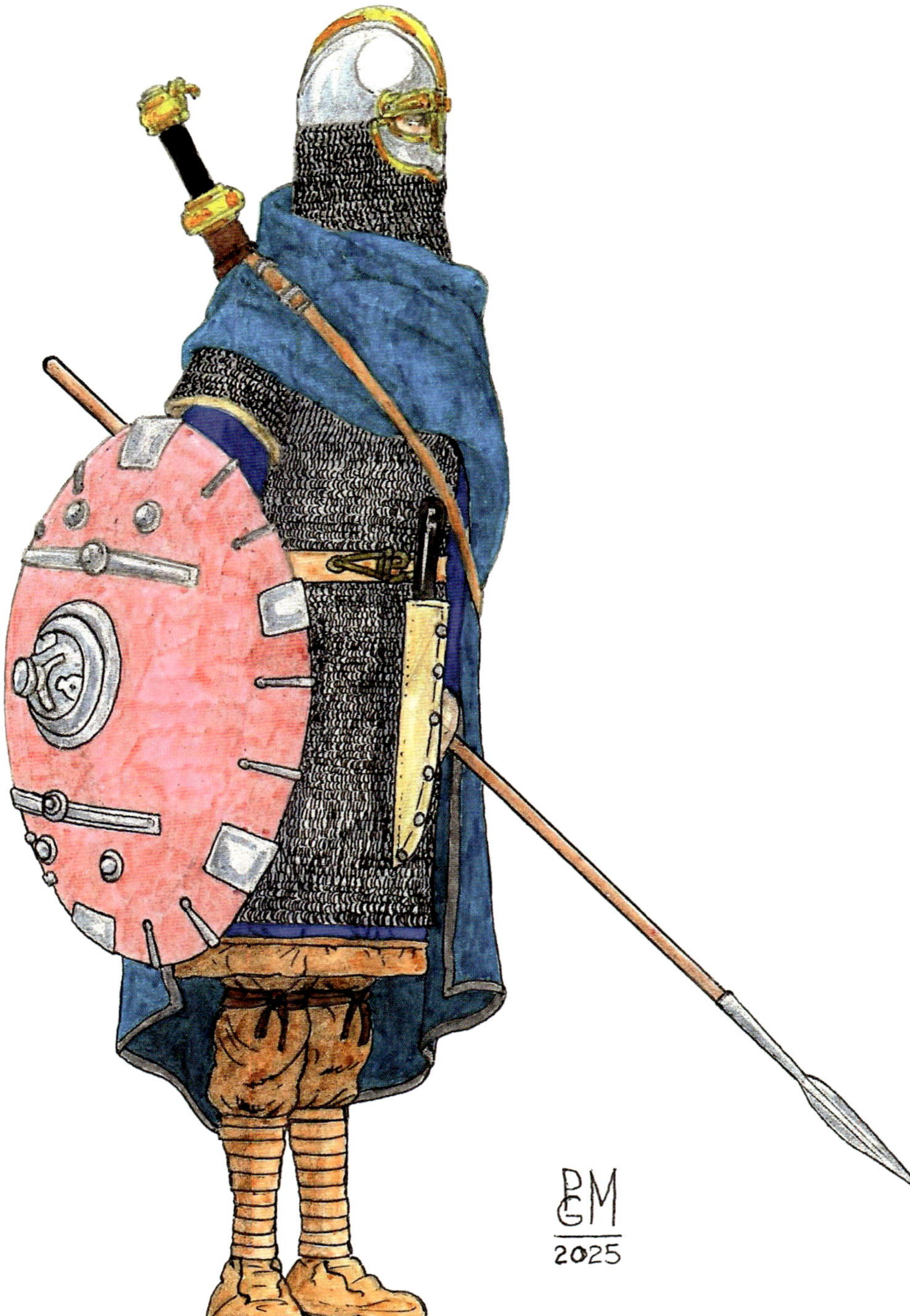

Saxon warrior wearing a helmet with facial mask in combination with his chainmail. (*Colour plate by Patricio Greve Moller, copyright of Gabriele Esposito*)

Saxon warrior wearing protective segments of metal armour on the forearms and on the shanks. (*Photo and copyright by Lindsay Kerr of Wulfheodenas*)

cap was usually covered with fur in the northern regions of the Empire. During the Crisis of the Third Century, all the various kinds of helmet traditionally worn by Roman soldiers were progressively abandoned and substituted with new ones. This happened mainly for two reasons. Firstly, because the previous models of helmet were quite elaborate to produce, requiring particular skills in order to be made. In an age of anarchy, characterized by the collapse of the military supply system, mass production required helmets with simpler designs. The second factor was the influence of the Sarmatians and Sassanids, the Romans learning from their new enemies how to produce cheaper and simpler models of helmet. These are commonly divided into two large families: ridge helmets and spangenhelms.

Ridge helmets are so-called because they were characterized by a bowl made up of two or four parts, united by a longitudinal ridge. This method of construction was copied by the Romans from Sassanid helmets. The earliest confirmed example of a Roman ridge helmet is the Richborough helmet, which dates back to AD 280. Differently from earlier Roman helmets, the skull of the ridge helmet was constructed from more than one element. Roman ridge helmets can be classified into two types of skull construction: bipartite and quadripartite, respectively referred to as Intercisa-type and Berkasovo-type. Bipartite construction was characterized by a two-part bowl united by a central ridge (running from front to back) and by the presence of small cheekpieces. It lacked a base-ring running around the rim of the bowl. Some surviving examples of the bipartite construction have metal crests, such as the helmets known as Intercisa-IV and River Maas. Quadripartite construction featured a four-piece bowl connected by a central ridge, with two plates (connected by a reinforcing band) on each side of the ridge and a base-ring uniting the elements of the skull at the rim of the helmet. This type of helmet was further characterized by large cheekpieces. Some surviving examples of quadripartite construction also have a nasal. It is believed that the cheekpieces were attached to the skull of the helmet by a liner and that a separate neck guard was frequently attached to the back of the helmet by flexible leather straps. Bipartite construction or Intercisa-type helmets have ear holes, while quadripartite construction or Berkasovo-type examples do not. Some scholars, bearing in mind that earlier Roman cavalry helmets usually had cheek guards with a section covering the ears, have suggested that the Intercisa-type was used by infantrymen and the Berkasovo-type by cavalrymen. This interesting hypothesis is supported by an important archaeological find, the Deurne helmet, which has an inscription related to a cavalry unit of the *Equites stablesiani*. However, both types of ridge helmet are depicted in several works of art as being worn by both infantry and cavalry. It is thus highly probable that they were used interchangeably.

Saxon warrior equipped with spear and round shield; the latter's surface is decorated with many decorative applications made of metal. (*Photo and copyright by Lindsay Kerr of Wulfheodenas*)

The spangenhelm arrived in Europe by way of what is now southern Russia and Ukraine, being spread by nomadic peoples like the Sarmatians, who lived in the Eurasian steppes. However, the term 'spangenhelm' is clearly of Germanic origins: 'spangen' refers to the metal strips that form the framework of the helmet, while 'helm' simply means 'helmet'. The characteristic metal strips of a spangenhelm

Saxon warrior armed with spear, sword and seax short sword.
(*Colour plate by Patricio Greve Moller, copyright of Gabriele Esposito*)

connect three to six steel or bronze plates, which made up a framework that has a conical design, curving with the shape of the head and culminating in a point. The front of the helmet generally included a nasal. Spangenhelms could also incorporate chainmail as neck protection, forming a sort of aventail at the back. Some surviving examples also include eye protection, having a shape that resembles modern eyeglass frames, whereas others have a full face mask. Older spangenhelms often had cheek flaps made from metal or leather. In general terms, the spangenhelm offered effective protection for the head and was relatively easy to produce. Both the new families of Roman helmets could have heavy decorations, especially if a helmet belonged to a rich officer. Many surviving examples of helmets from the Middle Empire have evidence of decorative silvering or are covered by costly silver-gilt sheathing. The job of decorating helmets was entrusted to special artisans working in the state factories, who were known as *barbaricarii*. Some helmets of senior officers, such as the Berkasovo-I helmet, were decorated with several glass gems (located on the bowl, on the cheekpieces and on the neckguard).

With the Constitutio Antoniana of AD 212, the main social distinction between legionaries and auxiliaries was suddenly cancelled: all the inhabitants of the Empire became Roman citizens and there was no more sense in the differences of equipment carried by legionaries and auxiliaries. Until the Crisis of the Third Century, legionaries were equipped with segmented armour known as *lorica segmentata*, while auxiliaries had traditional chainmail armour (*lorica hamata*). The Crisis of the Third Century marked a real turning point for Roman armour, with *lorica segmentata*, complex and difficult to produce, abandoned during the turbulent decades following AD 235. Traditional segmented armour is still reproduced on the Arch of Constantine, erected in AD 315, but these depictions are from an earlier monument erected by Marcus Aurelius and later incorporated into the Arch of Constantine. *Lorica segmentata* probably disappeared around the middle of the third century. It was replaced by the *lorica hamata* formerly worn only by auxiliaries, which started to be used by all units. The basic features of Roman chainmail remained more or less the same. It comprised alternating rows of closed washer-like rings punched from iron sheets and rows of riveted rings made from drawn wire that ran horizontally. These produced very flexible, reliable and strong armour. Each ring had an inner diameter of about 5mm and an outer diameter of about 7mm. Up to 30,000 rings went into each suit of *lorica hamata*, with an estimated production time of two months. In most cases, *lorica hamata* covered from the legs to the knees; its sleeves could be long or short. However, *lorica hamata* was not the only kind of armour worn by soldiers of the Middle Empire, there being three other three kinds which had very different origins and features. The first of these was the already popular *lorica squamata*, or scale

Saxon warrior wearing a helmet with facial mask. (*Photo by Viveka Sjölund, copyright by Uttaharjar*)

Saxon warrior armed with spear, sword and seax short sword. (*Photo by Viveka Sjölund, copyright by Uttaharjar*)

armour, that was made from small metal scales sewn to a fabric backing. Individual scales (*squamae*) could be of iron or bronze. The metal was generally not very thick, commonly just 0.5–0.8mm. Since the scales overlapped in every direction, however, the multiple layers gave good protection. Scales could have rounded, pointed or flat bottoms, with the corners clipped off at an angle. They could be flat, slightly domed or have a raised midrib/edge. The scales were wired or laced together in horizontal rows that were then laced or sewn to the backing. Each scale thus had between four and twelve: two or more at each side for wiring to the next scale in the row, one or two at the top for fastening to the backing, and sometimes one or two at the bottom to secure the scales to the backing or to each other. Occasionally the *squamae* could be tinned.

The second kind of armour used by the Roman Army of the Middle Empire was the lamellar type, which was employed on a much smaller scale than those discussed previously, being imported into Europe from the steppes of Eurasia only during the very last decades of the Middle Empire. It was mostly worn by mercenary *buccellarii* or by *foederati*, and not by actual Roman soldiers. Lamellar armour consisted of small platelets commonly known as lamellae, which were punched and laced together in order to be assembled in several horizontal rows. The lamellae could be made of metal, leather or horn; metal ones could be lacquered in order to resist corrosion or as decoration. Differently from scale armour, lamellar armour was not attached to a cloth or leather backing. The third type of armour was the model of cuirass commonly known as the muscle cuirass. During the Middle Empire, simpler versions of this type were usually preferred, with the sculpted anatomy reduced to an abstract design. The cuirasses of senior officers were often highly ornamented with sculpted mythological scenes or similar kinds of rich decorations. The muscle cuirass was mostly worn by officers, being considered a sign of their rank. Since the days of the Praetorians, the muscle cuirass had been the favourite kind of protection worn by all Roman guard units, a general trend that apparently continued. Generally speaking, neither light infantry nor light cavalry wore armour, while the heavy cavalry used the same kinds of armour described above for the foot troops.

During the course of the third century, the traditional *scutum* shield used by the legionaries disappeared, together with *lorica segmentata*. Mass production of the *scutum* was a complex process, with various phases needed to create a shield of good quality. As with other components of the standard Roman military equipment, manufacture of the rectangular shield proved unsustainable for the production structures and supply system of the Empire during the chaotic years of the third century. As a result, by the time of Constantine, almost all Roman units had adopted a new and simpler model of oval shield. This was carried by light infantry and cavalry too, although with some variations in its size (the shields of light infantry and cavalry were generally smaller than those of the heavy infantry, having a more circular shape). Differently from the *scutum*, the new oval shield was not convex but could be either dished (bowl-shaped) or flat. The oval/round shield was much larger than the *scutum* and was constructed in a different way: it was made of solid planks instead of plywood and was supported by a double grip (at the elbow and hand, whereas the *scutum* had just a single central grip). The general features of the oval/round shield made it much easier to produce than the previous rectangular one. In many respects, it was the direct heir of the oval shield used by the *auxilia* for their entire history. The new oval shield was about 110cm high and 90cm wide, being constructed with 1cm-thick wood planks, and was covered and bound with leather. A hollow iron or bronze boss covered the central hand grip. The *scutum* was usually painted with standard decorations, which were almost identical for each legion, and the shields of the auxiliaries were also generally painted with standard motifs. However, it was not possible to distinguish one unit from another thanks to the decorations on its shields. After the reforms of Diocletian and Constantine, the new oval/round shield started to be painted with different motifs according to the various units. Each formation of the Roman Army was now given its distinctive shield emblem. This was quite revolutionary, reflecting a very precise unit organization. Shield emblems of the Late Roman Army can be reconstructed thanks to the exceptional primary source the *Notitia Dignitatum*, although the motifs of some categories of troops have not survived in this and thus have been lost. Only the mobile *comitatenses* units had distinctive emblems painted on their shields; they could operate in various regions of the Empire, so needed to be identified by commanders of the field armies. As the limitanei served only in their home territories, they had no need to be identified through their shield emblems.

While the Roman legionaries of the Early Empire had excellent defensive equipment, comprising *lorica segmentata* and the *scutum*, the real strength of the Roman heavy infantry consisted of their offensive weapons: the *pilum* (heavy javelin), *gladius* (short sword) and *pugio* (dagger). The first weapon to be used in battle was the *pilum*, a javelin specifically designed to kill enemies from long distances or to limit them in the use of their shields (the *pilum* was extremely difficult to remove after striking a shield or cuirass). Once the enemy ranks had been shattered by the initial rain of javelins, the legionaries drew their short swords and charged their opponents. According to Roman tactical doctrine, emphasis was placed on using the *scutum* to provide maximum body coverage, while the *gladius* was used to attack with deadly thrusts and short cuts. These tactics helped the Romans to defeat any enemy infantry for centuries, while this kind of warfare also limited the number of casualties suffered by imperial troops. Using their swords to thrust in the few spaces created between the

Saxon warrior wearing a padded tunic. (*Photo and copyright by Lindsay Kerr of Wulfheodenas*)

Saxon warriors from the early phase of the Germanic conquest of Britain.
(Photo by Viveka Sjölund, copyright by Uttaharjar)

shields of their close formations, the legionaries were rarely exposed to the offensive weapons of their enemies, who had very few opportunities to manoeuvre. Like the *gladius*, the *pugio* dagger was a short stabbing weapon. It was used as a secondary arm during the most intense hand-to-hand fighting, especially when space for movement became very limited or when the *gladius* could not be used for any reason. Soon after the outset of the Crisis of the Third Century, the traditional Roman system of offensive weapons started to be completely modified. The short stabbing *gladius* designed for close-quarter fighting was gradually phased out by the new *spatha*, a long sword that had originally been used only by cavalrymen. At the same time, the *pugio* was gradually abandoned as secondary hand weapon, being replaced by simpler short and single-edged knives (which, unlike the *pugio*, were not carried by all soldiers on a regular basis).

The adoption of the *spatha* as the universal sword of the Roman Army was one of the many important military changes happening during the third century: Roman tactics were slowly changing due to the new threats faced by the Empire. The recent prominence of cavalry had transformed the Roman Army into a highly mobile force mostly composed of heavily armoured horsemen and mounted archers. As a result of cavalry's predominance on the fields of battle, close infantry formations designed for hand-to-hand fighting were slowly abandoned, with the long slashing swords of the cavalry starting to be employed by the infantry too. The cavalry's long sword had been copied by the Romans from the Celts; similarly, the *gladius* had been copied from the Iberian warriors of Hannibal who fought against Rome during the Punic Wars. The *spatha* was introduced into the Roman Army by the auxiliary cavalry units comprising Celtic recruits from Gaul. Generally speaking, the units of *auxilia* retained their own weapons and fighting traditions after joining the Roman Army. The Celtic cavalry, famed for their excellent long swords, obviously continued to use these weapons. As a result, from the early days of the Empire, the Celtic *spatha* started to be used by the majority of the Roman cavalry units. The straight and long sword had a standard blade length of between 0.75 and 1 metre, making it much longer than the *gladius*. After being used for several decades only by the cavalry, the *spatha* also started to be employed by the heavy infantry, the *gladius* initially being relegated to use as a light infantry weapon and soon being totally abandoned. The *spatha* thus started to be produced in two different versions, one for infantry and one for cavalry. The infantry version had a long point, while that for the cavalry had a rounded tip that prevented accidental stabbing of the cavalryman's foot. From the days of the Early Empire, the Roman legionary's fighting style had been defined by two weapons: the *pilum* and the *gladius*. The *pilum*, a javelin with a long iron shank for punching through enemy shields and armour, was usually thrown at close range. It gave the Roman legionaries a great tactical advantage over their enemies, being a very effective light infantry weapon in the hands of heavily armoured infantrymen. No other soldier in the Mediterranean world had such an excellent defensive equipment used together with a deadly missile weapon like the *pilum*.

The traditional heavy *pilum* was gradually abandoned from around AD 250, during the Crisis of the Third Century. Differently from other pieces of traditional Roman military equipment, it was not substituted by a single new weapon: the Roman infantrymen of the Middle Empire could use two different kinds of javelin to break up the ranks of the enemy. Both these new missile weapons, known as the *spiculum* (heavy javelin) and *verutum* (light javelin), had butt-spikes that protected the base of the shaft from rot and could also be used for thrusting. The *spiculum* replaced the *pilum* as the heavy infantryman's main throwing weapon. Scholars suppose that it could have resulted from the gradual combination of the *pilum* with the standard Germanic javelin, known as the *angon*. The latter was quite similar to (and probably derived from) the *pilum*, having a barbed head and a long narrow socket or shank made of iron mounted on a wooden haft. The barbs were designed to lodge into enemy shields so that it could not be removed, while the long iron shank prevented the head from being cut from the shaft. The *angon* was likely designed like the *pilum* for the purpose of disabling enemy shields, leaving combatants vulnerable and disrupting enemy formations. The shaft may have been decorated, and iron or bronze rings were sometimes fitted onto it, which may have marked the centre of balance and thus the best place to hold the weapon. The Roman *spiculum* had all the main features of the Germanic *angon*: the main difference between the *spiculum* and the *pilum* was the length of the thin point, the new javelin tending to have a much shorter point than the previous one. The *spiculum* was significantly shorter than its predecessor, being around 190cm long. Its exact design is not fully known, there being many variants, but it had a medium iron shank attached to the head.

In addition to the *spiculum*, soldiers of the Middle Empire could also be armed with a lighter and longer-ranged javelin, the verutum. This was the main missile weapon of light infantry and cavalry, but could also be used by heavy infantrymen in combination with the *spiculum*. The *verutum* had been used for skirmishing purposes since the days of the Republic, being issued to the light infantry of the legions. During the Crisis of the Third Century, however, it started to be employed by all kinds of units. The shaft of the *verutum* was about 1.1 metres long, much shorter than the *pilum*. The point measured about 13cm, and each *verutum* had either an iron shank like the *spiculum* or a tapering metal head. The *verutum* had a narrow armour-piercing head similar to that of the heavy javelins, though obviously with inferior penetration. Over time, it seems that the *spiculum* started to be used less widely apparently being

Saxon warlord wearing a helmet of the Vendel XIV model. (*Photo by Viveka Sjölund, copyright by Uttaharjar*)

Saxon warrior armed with sword. (*Photo by Viveka Sjölund, copyright by Uttaharjar*)

replaced by the *verutum* as the main javelin for heavy infantry. Soldiers of the Middle Empire could also be armed with innovative missile weapons known as *plumbatae* or *martiobarbuli*. These were lead-weighted darts, usually carried by the heavy infantry on the back of their oval shields and then thrown. They were like a short arrow with a weight attached to the shaft. The term *plumbatae* etymologically contains the word *plumbum*', which means 'lead' in Latin, so the term *plumbatae* could be translated as 'lead-weighted darts'. *Martiobarbuli* is most likely an assimilation of the words *martio* and *barbuli*, so it can be translated as 'little barbs of Mars'. This second etymology clearly implies a barbed head. An important archaeological find from Wroxeter in Shropshire finally confirmed the general picture that existed of the *plumbatae*: fletched darts with an iron head, weighted with lead. They had little penetrating power and a very short range (just 30 metres), but their barbed heads made them effective for crippling an enemy or his horse without armour. Each heavy infantryman carried six of them clipped to the back of his shield.

After the reforms of Gaius Marius, the Roman heavy infantry had abandoned the spear as one of its main offensive weapons, with all legionaries started to be equipped with the *pilum*. The infantry of the auxiliary units did not receive the *pilum* and continued to have the normal model of spear (*lancea*). As we have seen, the legionaries started to abandon the *pilum* around AD 250; this was replaced by the new *spiculum* as a heavy javelin, but a good number of legionaries started to have the *lancea* of the auxiliaries as their main weapon. As a result, after several centuries, the Roman heavy infantry was again equipped with spears on a large scale. The *lancea* of the Middle Empire was a little different from that previously employed by the auxiliaries: it was light enough to be thrown just prior to contact but could be retained for use in hand-to-hand combat. Apparently, judging from the primary sources that are available, the heavy infantrymen of the Middle Empire preferred using the *lancea* for close fighting, while usually carrying two or three *spicula* to be used as throwing weapons. Often, however, a legionary could be armed only with a *lancea*, while the soldiers of the *auxilia palatina*, being elite light infantry, obviously were mostly equipped with the *spiculum* or the *verutum* (the latter being the standard weapon of all light infantrymen and light cavalrymen). Although this was the situation for heavy infantry spears, it should be borne in mind that the Roman cavalry had always continued to use spears. During the Crisis of the Third Century, however, the Roman heavy cavalry abandoned the traditional model of *lancea* and replaced it with a new one known as the *contus*.

The *contus* was a type of long wooden lance, originally used by the Iranian heavy cavalry. From the first century AD, this weapon had started to be employed on a massive scale by the Sarmatians. It was later adopted also by the Parthian heavy

Saxon warrior equipped with helmet and chainmail. (*Colour plate by Patricio Greve Moller, copyright of Gabriele Esposito*)

Saxon warrior armed with spear and seax short sword.
(*Colour plate by Patricio Greve Moller, copyright of Gabriele Esposito*)

cavalry, who used it against the Romans. The *contus* was about 4 metres long and had to be wielded with two hands while controlling the horse using the knees; this made it a specialist weapon that required much training and good horsemanship to use. Initially, only highly trained cavalrymen such as those fielded by the Sassanids could use the weapon effectively. The *contus* was reputedly a weapon of great power, compared to other cavalry spears of the time. The great length of the lance was probably the origin of its name, since the Greek word *kontus* means 'oar' or 'barge-pole'. Roman cavalry began wielding the *contus* on a large scale after facing the Sarmatian heavy cavalry in battle. The light cavalry, meanwhile, continued to be armed with normal *verutum* javelins. From their nomadic Sarmatian enemies, the Romans also adopted a new kind of military standard, the draco. This was introduced into the Roman cavalry by Sarmatian auxiliaries during the second half of the second century AD. Apparently, it soon proved very successful and was later adopted by infantry units too. In the infantry, it substituted the traditional *vexillum* as the standard of the cohort, the *Vexillifer* of each cohort being replaced by a *Draconarius*. The eagle remained the primary symbol of the legions. The draco was a traditional element of Dacian military equipment, being later adopted by the Sarmatians, who passed its use to the Romans. As is suggested by its name, it had the form of a dragon, with open, wolf-like jaws containing several metal tongues. The hollow head of the dragon was made of metal and was mounted on a pole, and had a long fabric tube affixed at the rear. When in use, the draco was held up into the wind, where it filled with air and made a shrill sound as the wind passed through its metal tongues. As a consequence, in addition to being a military standard, it was also a psychological weapon that resembled a terrifying dragon.

During the Early Empire, the Roman Army always included a large number of light infantrymen equipped as slingers. These were initially mercenaries but were later auxiliaries from the Balearic Islands, who had an ancient military tradition that was strongly linked to the use of the sling as a skirmishing weapon. Over time, however, slings started to be used by soldiers from every corner of the Empire. Meanwhile, a new type of sling started to be used alongside the original model traditionally employed in the Balearic Islands. The slingers of Constantine's time were mostly equipped with the staff sling, which consisted of a staff (a length of wood) with a short sling at one end. One cord of the sling was firmly attached to the staff, while the other end had a loop that slid off to release the projectile. Staff slings were extremely powerful, as the staff could be as long as 2 metres, creating a powerful lever. Ancient art shows slingers holding staff slings by one end, with the pocket behind them, using both hands to throw the staves forward over their heads. The staff sling could throw heavy projectiles a much greater distance and at a higher arc than a traditional hand sling, and could be just as accurate in the hands of an experienced skirmisher. Archers were always a secondary element of the Roman Army during the Early Empire. The bow was not an important weapon in the Roman military tradition, and all units of archers employed by the Empire were composed of provincial auxiliaries. With the cavalry reforms of the third century, however, the Romans started to equip some of their cavalry as mounted archers, on the model of the Sarmatian and Sassanid horsemen. As a result, the Roman light cavalry adopted the composite bow of the Eurasian steppes as one of its primary weapons. At the same time, large numbers of light infantry units started to be defined as *sagittarii*, being equipped with bows of the traditional wooden model employed in continental Europe.

The composite bow was made from horn, wood and sinew laminated together. The horn was on the belly facing the archer, while sinew was on the outer side of the wooden core. It was the wooden core that gave the bow its shape and dimensional stability. When the bow was drawn, the sinew (stretched on the outside) and the horn (compressed on the inside) stored more energy than wood for the same length of bow. The construction of a composite bow was a very complex process, requiring more varieties of material than a

Saxon warrior wearing the skin of a wolf over his shoulders. (*Photo and copyright by Lindsay Kerr of Wulfheodenas*)

Saxon warrior bearing a standard. (*Photo and copyright by Lindsay Kerr of Wulfheodenas*)

wooden bow and much more time. It was often made of multiple pieces, joined with animal glue in V-splices. Pieced construction allowed the use of woods with different mechanical properties for the bending and non-bending sections: the wood of the bending part of the limb had to endure intense shearing stress. A thin layer of horn was glued onto what would be the belly of the bow; this could store more energy than wood in compression. Goat and sheep horn was commonly used for this purpose. The sinew, soaked in animal glue, was then laid in layers on the back of the bow, the strands of sinew being oriented along the length of the bow. The sinew was normally obtained from the lower legs and back of wild deer or domestic ungulates. Sinew would extend farther than wood, again allowing more energy storage. Hide glue was used to attach layers of sinew to the back of the bow and to fix the horn belly to the wooden core. The animal glue could lose strength in humid conditions and be quickly ruined by rain or submersion in water, so composite bows were always stored in protective leather cases. The wooden bow of the infantry, the *arcubus ligneis*, was constructed according to the longbow tradition of continental Europe from a single piece of wood. Crafting a composite bow could take a week's work, plus a drying time of several months, while a wooden bow could be made in one day and dried in a week. The main advantage of composite bows over longbows was their combination of smaller size with higher power. In addition, almost all composite bows are recurved, as their shape curves away from the archer. This design gives higher draw-weight in the early stages of the archer's draw, thereby storing more total energy. The method used by Roman mounted archers to carry arrows showed a clear nomadic influence, as they were held pointing upwards in a barrel quiver hanging from the waistbelt, but infantry quivers were round-bottomed cylinders hanging from a shoulder-strap.

Chapter 9

Saxon Military Organization and Weapons

The basis of the Anglo-Saxons' military organization, since the early days of the Germanic settlement in England, was the obligation of every able-bodied freeman aged between 15 and 60 to perform military service. When mobilized for war, the Anglo-Saxon men made up the *fyrd*, which was the standard army deployed by Anglo-Saxon monarchs during the early decades of their settlement in England. The *fyrd* could be mobilized to defend the homeland of its members from foreign attack or to join a royal expedition aimed at invading enemy territory. In the first case, all able-bodied freemen of a tribal group were required to give their personal contribution; in the second case, only some members of each tribal group were chosen to serve under the orders of the king. The *fyrd* was a general levy and thus was in common – with different denominations – with all the Germanic peoples migrating across Late Roman Europe. Service in the *fyrd* was usually of short duration and had practically no costs for the Anglo-Saxon kings, because the members of a general levy were expected to provide their own arms and provisions and were not paid by the monarch for their military service. Originally, the *fyrd* was mobilized and organized on a local basis, according to the tribal subdivisions of the various groups, thus working as a sort of regional levy. The *fyrd* armies consisted almost entirely of infantry, with most of their members fighting on foot. With the progression of time, the various *fyrd* armies started to be mobilized and recruited on a shire basis, which improved their level of cohesion but did not radically change their combat capabilities. The creation of the shires and the modification of the *fyrd* system took place after the establishment of the Heptarchy, when the tribal Anglo-Saxon groups that settled in England started to be transformed into kingdoms.

Military service at the order of the monarch was compulsory, with fines having to be paid by those freemen who did not carry it out. If a nobleman holding lands neglected military service, he had to forfeit his land and pay a fine of 120 shillings; a nobleman without land properties had to pay 60 shillings and a commoner had to pay 30 shillings. It was the responsibility of each shire *fyrd* to deal with small raids and incursions conducted on a local scale, while in the event of large-scale foreign invasions it was the king's responsibility to call up the national *fyrd* that was made up of all the able-bodied men of his realm. Conditions of service for the

Saxon warlord wearing a corselet of scale armour. (*Colour plate by Patricio Greve Moller, copyright of Gabriele Esposito*)

Saxon warrior armed with spear, sword, seax and dagger. (*Photo and copyright by Lindsay Kerr of Wulfheodenas*)

national *fyrd* (also known as the great *fyrd*) and for the shire *fyrd* were quite different, since in most cases the Anglo-Saxon commoners were not particularly happy about the idea of serving under their king and far from their homes for long periods of time. Most of the Anglo-Saxon freemen were peasants, who spent most of their lives working in the fields and following the natural cycles of the land. As a result, on most occasions, service in the great *fyrd* lasted for one day only and a king had to pay his freemen if any additional days of service were needed. Anglo-Saxon men were much happier to serve in their shire *fyrd*, which was mostly tasked with defending their own properties. The local *fyrds* recruited from the shires that were located on the borders of a kingdom were used to conducting offensive operations against foreign communities living on their tract of frontier, usually being mobilized for a period of fifteen days without receiving any pay from the royal administration. Due to the situation described above, most Anglo-Saxon kings assembled their armies without calling up the great *fyrd*. On most occasions, only one freeman from each 5 hides of land was required to serve and to join the national *fyrd* that was mobilized for a campaign. The selected individual was expected to be equipped with a spear and shield, to have provisions for two months and to receive a wage of 4 shillings, provided by the hides from which he was levied. The provisions and wage were supplied by the other landholders who made up the 5-hides unit in proportion to the land they held. The size of a hide varied from region to region, but was generally deemed the extent of land needed to sustain a household. The kingdoms of the Angles used *carucates* as land units instead of hides, while the Jutes of Kent used *sulungs*.

A new social class of lesser noblemen gradually emerged from the Saxon communities and started to hold estates, the average size of which was 5 hides. This meant that the bulk of the select *fyrd* began to consist of minor landowners who considered military service an opportunity to increase their social position. These men were known as *thegns*, an Old English term meaning 'servant', 'attendant' or 'retainer'. It was commonly applied to the lesser aristocratic retainers of a king or of a senior nobleman (such as an ealdormen), who spent most of their lives serving as semi-professional soldiers. Germanic societies, including that of the Anglo-Saxons, had always comprised a class of semi-professional warriors who made up the *comitatus*, or 'military household', of a king or noble. One such armed retainer was commonly known as a *gesith* and was a personal friend/retainer of an important warlord. After settling in England, the Anglo-Saxons started to replace the term *gesith* with the new *thegn*. Initially, the Germanic monarchs who invaded England could not count on large numbers of armed retainers, since they still had to conquer enough lands to create a proper aristocracy of landowners. Over time, however, an increasing number of minor nobles started to emerge, meaning the number of *thegns* was greatly expanded.

A minor landowner could be a king's *thegn* (a semi-professional soldier serving under the direct orders of his monarch) or a median *thegn* (who served an earl). The *thegns* had a very important military function, gradually becoming the backbone of the Saxon armies. They had to serve their king or earl, but were also required to enforce the military service of the other men living on their estates and to take command of the shire *fyrds* when they were mobilized. The co-existence of *thegns* and *fyrdmen* created a semi-permanent militia organization: the king and the major nobles had a certain number of semi-professional soldiers (*thegns*) in each shire, and these – in case of need – were tasked with mobilizing and commanding the non-professional soldiers (*fyrdmen*) of each local community. If no *thegn* was present within a 5-hides unit, military service in the select *fyrd* was performed by one of the upper-class peasants. These were known as *cnichts*, while the poorest peasants were called *ceorls*. Some semi-professional warriors inherited the rank of *thegn* from their fathers, while others acquired it through property ownership or wealth. The number of *thegns* continued to increase, thanks to the general improvement in living conditions that took place in Saxon England. As a result, in addition to the king's *thegn* and the medium *thegn*, a new third category of semi-professional soldiers was introduced: the common *thegn*. This consisted of middle-status local nobles who were too weak to become earls but too strong to be simple retainers of the king or an earl.

In addition to the *fyrdmen* and the *thegns*, since the time of their arrival in England, Anglo-Saxon armies always comprised small numbers of elite household troops that were made up of professional soldiers. These warriors, known as *hearthweru*, were loyal companions or followers of a king who protected him by acting as a bodyguard. The *hearthweru* were the means by which an Anglo-Saxon warlord imposed his will over his subjects and enjoyed a privileged status of full-time warriors. They spent most of their lives improving their combat skills and initially made up the bulk of the fighting forces fielded by the Anglo-Saxon kings. Most of the early Germanic expeditions directed against Britain only consisted of between three and five longships, each transporting sixty *hearthweru* warriors each. In the early decades of the Anglo-Saxon settlement in England, the personal retinues of warlords played a prominent military role in operations against the Britons. The personal warbands of the Anglo-Saxon warlords founded the future royal houses of the Heptarchy, their members becoming the future earls or high-ranking aristocrats of the Anglo-Saxon realms. Generally speaking, the early Anglo-Saxon armies were very small, with any armed group with more than thirty-five warriors being defined as a *heer*, or 'army'. After the Anglo-Saxon settlement in England became more stable one and the military system based on the *fyrds* was established, the small retinues of professional *hearthweru* warriors – known as *hirds* – continued to exist but lost most of their original importance.

The everyday dress of an Anglo-Saxon warrior was exactly the same as that worn by the free males of all the Germanic kingdoms that were created after the fall of the Roman Empire. It consisted of two main elements: cloak and tunic. The cloak was rectangular in shape, being about 2.5 metres long and 1.5 metres wide. Made of woollen yarn, it was usually pinned at the right shoulder and hung to about knee-length. Each cloak was kept in position with a metal brooch known as a *fibula*, which could be produced in many different patterns. When the Anglo-Saxons arrived in England, most of their brooches were cruciform and had a bowed section in order to allow material to be pulled through between the body of the wearer and the back-mounted pin. New and smaller brooches having a simple circular shape became increasingly popular. The tunic, like the cloak, was made of woollen yarn; it was usually worn belted at the waist in such a way as to raise the hem to the knees. Sometimes, however, tunics could be worn without a belt, with their hems hanging to the calves. Most of the Anglo-Saxon tunics had long sleeves that reached well down over the fingers, but were usually worn pulled or folded back to the wrist during hot months. The neck of each tunic had either a square or circular opening for the head, generally reinforced with a coloured placket. This opening could be closed either by a drawstring or a brooch/bead. Cloaks and tunics could be produced in a variety of bright colours, although plain hues were extremely popular among the common warriors. Aristocratic warlords wore garments heavily ornamented with coloured plackets and/or decorative embroidering on the edges. Leggings were quite common during the early years of the Anglo-Saxon presence in England, usually taking the form of trousers with the feet sewn into them and slits at the ankles that allowed them to be put on more easily. Over time, separate leggings and hose became increasingly popular, with trousers that were sometimes allowed to hang loose around the ankles. Quite frequently, long fabric strips could be wound closely to the calf, acting as puttees. These were popular for campaign use, but could also be worn during everyday life. The leg bindings were known as *winniga* and usually covered most of the leg, protecting both the leg and trousers from cold and dirt. The footwear of the Anglo-Saxons was very simple, consisting of shoes made of cow hide. All the belts worn by Anglo-Saxon warriors were made of leather and were generally about 2.5cm wide. The buckles and strap-ends of belts were made of copper alloy and could be heavily decorated if worn by aristocratic warlords. The standard headgear of Anglo-Saxon men was the Phrygian Cap, which was made of wool or felt. It had a characteristic forward-drooping peak and had been a symbol of free status since the days of the Roman Empire. The Phrygian Cap was used as fatigue headgear by commoners, but was popular too among nobles, who wore decorated versions.

Saxon warrior equipped with axe and round shield.
(*Colour plate by Patricio Greve Moller, copyright of Gabriele Esposito*)

Saxon warlord armed with sword. (*Photo and copyright by Lindsay Kerr of Wulfheodenas*)

Warriors of the Germanic nations, including the Anglo-Saxons, threw their weapons into swamps as offerings in thanks for a military victory or in fulfilment of vows made to the gods. As a result of this ceremonial practice, archaeologists have been able to discover many pieces of Anglo-Saxon military equipment across Denmark and England. Around a fifth of Anglo-Saxon male burials contain weapons, so excavations conducted in burial sites have also been fundamental to determine the main features of offensive and defensive equipment employed by Anglo-Saxon warriors. Two particular archaeological finds have been essential for understanding the composition of the Anglo-Saxons' military panoply: those of Benty Grange (1848) and Sutton Hoo (1939). Both these finds were extremely important, especially regarding defensive equipment, comprising spectacular and highly decorated helmets. The Benty Grange helmet, unearthed in Derbyshire, is famous because of the small boar at its apex, which is described in some passages of the famous Anglo-Saxon poem *Beowulf*. It was constructed by covering the outside of an iron framework with plates of horn and the inside with leather. That found at Benty Grange was the first Anglo-Saxon helmet to be discovered in England and was followed by just another five ones, each of which was named after the location of its finding: Sutton Hoo (in Suffolk), York, Wollaston (Northamptonshire), Shorwell (Isle of Wight) and Staffordshire.

The Benty Grange helmet is part of the large family of crested helmets, which were a Germanic improved version of the Late Roman ridge helmets. The latter were characterized by having a bowl made up of two or four parts, united by a longitudinal ridge. Those of bipartite construction featured a two-part bowl united by a central ridge (running from front to back) and had small cheekpieces. They lacked a base-ring running around the rim of the bowl. Those of quadripartite construction were characterized by a four-piece bowl connected by a central ridge, with two plates (connected by a reinforcing band) on each side of the ridge and a base-ring uniting the elements of the skull at the rim of the helmet. Once again, such helmets had cheekpieces. Both kinds of ridge helmet could have a nasal on the front. The cheekpieces were attached to the skull of the helmet by a liner, and very frequently a separate neck guard was attached to the back of the helmet by flexible leather straps. Bipartite construction examples had ear holes, while quadripartite versions did not. The most striking feature of the Benty Grange helmet is the decorative boar on its apex. This pagan symbol faces towards a Christian cross placed on the nasal, making it a perfect example of the Anglo-Saxons' early syncretism. The Sutton Hoo helmet is considered the most beautiful work of art produced by the Anglo-Saxons in England, thanks to its magnificent and complex decorations. It is widely believed to have belonged to King Raedwald of East Anglia, its elaborate ornamentations probably giving it a secondary ceremonial function akin to that of a crown. Made of iron and covered with decorated sheets of tinned bronze, it has fluted strips of moulding dividing its exterior surface into panels, each of which is stamped with a different decorative design. On the front, the Sutton Hoo helmet has a magnificent facial mask comprising eyebrows, a nose and moustache. These decorated elements create the general image of a man, joined by a dragon's head to become a soaring dragon with outstretched wings.

The Staffordshire helmet, discovered in 2009, looks very similar to a Late Roman ridge helmet but its skull was made from a single piece of iron. On the outer surface it is covered with reliefs of silver gilt foil, closely resembling the panels of the Sutton Hoo helmet (each of them is stamped with a decorative design). The Staffordshire helmet has a nasal but no facial mask. The York helmet, also known as the Coppergate helmet, is made of iron and copper alloy and has many unique details. It features two low crests of brass: one running from front to back, the other from side to side. These form a distinctive cross shape when viewed from above. The brass banding within the crests bears a Latin inscription: 'In the name of our Lord Jesus, the Holy Spirit and God; and to all we say Amen, Oshere, Christ'. The brass crest running from front to back terminates at the front of the helmet with a decorative animal head placed at the base of the nasal. The brass eyebrow decorations flanking the nasal also terminate in animal heads. Cheekpieces and a mail aventail for protection of the neck complete the helmet. The Wollaston helmet, also known as the Pioneer helmet, was discovered fifteen years after the Staffordshire one (in 1997). It has the same basic form and characteristics as the latter, but has very little decoration and its skull is constructed from twelve individual components riveted together. On its apex, the Wollaston helmet has a small boar like the Benty Grange one; this was forged from a single rod of iron and was affixed to the nose-to-nape crest. The five helmets described above were all decorated and thus were likely all used by warlords. The simpler Shorwell helmet was presumably worn by a common warrior, since it was very cheap to produce. It was constructed from eight pieces of iron riveted together, including one brow band encircling the forehead and a long nose-to-nape band running from the front to the back. All the bands of the helmet featured thickened edges made by hammering the metal, while three copper alloy rivets were placed on the right side of the brow band and were probably used to attach a cheek guard made of leather. Differently from the other five Anglo-Saxon helmets found in England, the Shorwell one does not belong to the family of crested helmets, being of a different continental model that could be found in the lands of the Franks.

Although Anglo-Saxon written sources make frequent references to mail shirts or 'byrnies', only one example of early Anglo-Saxon chainmail has been discovered

Saxon warlord wearing a tunic made of leather.
(Photo and copyright by Lindsay Kerr of Wulfheodenas)

Saxon warrior armed with spear and sword. (*Photo by Viveka Sjölund, copyright by Uttaharjar*)

in England (at Sutton Hoo). Consequently, it is plausible to assume that until the arrival of the Vikings most Anglo-Saxon warriors did not wear armour. Indeed, only the richest warlords could afford a mail cuirass. Over time, this situation started to change, with an increasing number of professional Saxon warriors beginning to be equipped with chainmail. Each of these comprised alternating rows of closed washer-like rings punched from iron sheets and rows of riveted rings made from drawn wire that ran horizontally, producing very flexible, reliable and strong armour. Each ring had an inner diameter of about 5mm and an outer diameter of about 7mm. Up to 30,000 rings went into one chainmail, and the estimated production time for this type of cuirass was two months. Although labour intensive to manufacture, with good maintenance this kind of armour could be used for several decades by a warrior. Usually, the mail shirts covered the legs to the knees, and their sleeves could be long or short. During the early decades of their presence in England, it is highly probable that the Anglo-Saxons also used scale armour as an alternative to mail cuirasses. Germanic scale armour was made of small metal scales sewn to a fabric backing. Individual scales (*squamae*) could be of iron or bronze, and the scale cuirasses were very similar in composition and construction to the *lorica squamata* previously described for the armies of Rome's Middle Empire.

The most important component of an Anglo-Saxon warrior's defensive panoply was his shield. This had a distinctive round shape and was quite flat, having a hole in the middle where a wooden carrying handle was mounted crossways on the inside. A dome of plate iron, the boss, was nailed over the hole on the outside in order to protect the hand. The boss had the shape of a straight-sided cone with a flanged base. Four holes in the flange allowed the boss to be riveted to the shield's face. Decorative fittings made of copper alloy or gold could be applied on the external surface of the boss. Anglo-Saxon shields had a diameter of 80–95cm and were made up of seven or eight planks glued together, edge to edge, in order to form a single plate. The thickness of the planks was 7–8mm near the middle of the shield and 5–6mm near the edge. A layer of rawhide (usually cow hide) was glued onto the whole of the shield's front and back, held in position by stitch holes that were placed round the edge, where a band of rawhide was folded round and sewn for reinforcement. The rawhide reduced the risk of the wood splitting and helped in stopping enemy arrows. Linden softwood was usually chosen to construct shields, the average weight of which was 7kg. When not in combat, Anglo-Saxon warriors carried their shields on the back, using a leather belt that was attached to the wooden handle. Anglo-Saxon shields were frequently reinforced with an iron strip around the rim, which was particularly useful during hand-to-hand fighting. Most shields were painted in a single colour, but some could be decorated with specific designs. Simple crosses and sacred animals/creatures (for example crows or dragons) were the most common designs. Rich warlords frequently ornamented the outer surface of their shields with decorative fittings made of copper alloy or gold. The Anglo-Saxons were famed for the high quality of their weapons, which had a specific social function in England during the early Middle Ages: bearing arms was both a right and a duty of free men and distinguished them from slaves. As a result, weapons were status symbols, their quality and ornamentation reflecting the economic capabilities of their owner.

In the Anglo-Saxon world, swords were items of great symbolic value, as producing them was extremely difficult and costly. Only the most prominent warlords could have a sword of high quality, and such weapons were usually handed down from generation to generation. Most Anglo-Saxon warriors gave a name to their swords and had a special relationship with them, since they also acted as amulets and their symbolism was strongly linked to the very soul of their owner. Elegant shapes and rich ornamentations were typical of the aristocrats' weaponry, but even most middle-class warriors had no hesitation in spending large sums of money in order to have the best arms. In Anglo-Saxon England, the processes of forging and tempering were performed by specialized craftsmen and were surrounded by a web of myth: use of the best materials and control of the temperature during the various productive phases were vital in the creation of an effective weapon. Anglo-Saxon swords were often decorated with symbols having a religious or cultural meaning, which were reproduced as patterns that were laid into the iron during forging and became visible when the external surface of the weapon was polished and etched. A good sword blade had to be flexible but should not be easily broken. In addition, its edge had to keep its sharpness for as long as possible. These main characteristics were obtained by placing hard steel on the sword's edge and soft iron along the middle of the blade. Producing a sword of good quality was an extremely long process, which had several phases: forging, folding, hammering and forging again. Reworking steel and iron at high temperatures rendered them homogenous, reducing the risk of the weapon shattering under the strain of use. The Anglo-Saxon sword was a single-handed weapon that was designed to leave one of the warrior's hands free in order to hold his shield. Its hilt consisted of three parts: back-hilt, grip and fore-hilt. Sometimes the latter was made up of two parts, the hindmost one of which was commonly known as the pommel. Most of the hilts were made of iron, but sometimes they could be bronze. The total length of an Anglo-Saxon sword was of 80–85cm, while the average length of the blade was of 65–70cm. Blades were 4–5cm wide and their weight was restricted towards the point, which was done by tapering the blade both in breadth and thickness towards the point. Blade thickness was thus 6mm near the hilt and 2mm at the point of the sword. To reduce the weight further and increase flexibility,

Saxon warrior armed with spear.
(Photo by Viveka Sjölund, copyright by Uttaharjar)

Saxon warrior armed with spear, long seax and dagger. (*Colour plate by Patricio Greve Moller, copyright of Gabriele Esposito*)

a groove was forged and ground out along the middle of the blade. The centre of gravity of the weapon was near the hilt, making it easy to handle. Several Anglo-Saxon swords, especially those belonging to the richest individuals, had decorative inscriptions on the blade and decorated hilts. All swords were carried in leather-bound wooden scabbards that were suspended from a strap across the right shoulder. Like the scabbard, the hilt was made of an organic material such as horn or antler.

Most of the common Anglo-Saxon warriors did not have a sword, being equipped quite simply with just a spear and shield. Anglo-Saxon spears were produced in two main versions: throwing spears and thrusting spears. The heads of throwing spears had an average length of 20cm, while those thrusting spears had a standard length of 70cm. Spear heads consisted of two parts: the blade and the socket. The wooden shaft was fixed into the socket with one or two nails. Anglo-Saxon spears could also have two projections on the side of the socket, known as wings, which were used to ease the removal of the spear from enemy shields. Occasionally, the back end of the shaft was capped with a metal ferrule. Spear blades could be of two different kinds, the first of which was older than the second. The first model of blade was forged with a herringbone pattern along the middle and had curved edges, and blended inconspicuously into the socket. The socket tended to have a square internal cross-section and was decorated with longitudinal grooves. The second model of blade had nearly straight edges (which ended in an angle at the base) and a marked narrowing as it merged into the socket. This socket was round in cross-section and could be decorated with inlaid precious metal. Wings were very common on the first model and quite rare on the second. The wings had another important practical function, being used for hooking onto the edge of an enemy shield and opening the way to a strike at an adversary. The wooden shaft of thrusting spears was longer than that of throwing spears; the former was 2.5–3 metres long, while the latter was some 1.5 metres. The diameter of all shafts was about 2.5cm and sometimes narrowed towards the back end.

During the period of the great migrations, three new offensive weapons were added to the traditional panoply of Germanic warriors: the angon, the seax and the francisca. The angon was a heavy javelin with a barbed head and a long narrow socket or shank, which was made of iron and was mounted on a wooden haft. The barbs of the head were designed to lodge in enemy shields so that the javelin could not be removed, while the long iron shank prevented the head from being cut from the shaft. The angon was likely designed for the purpose of disabling enemy shields, thereby leaving enemy combatants vulnerable. Its shaft could be decorated, and sometimes iron or bronze rings were fitted onto it to mark the centre of balance, the best place to hold the weapon. The seax (also known as a scramasax) was a short sword from which the same term 'Saxons' probably derived. Its name meant 'knife' in Germanic language. The seax had a large and single-edged blade with a tang in the centre, inserted into an organic hilt made of wood or horn. Its total length was 70–90cm, while the handle was 15–25cm long and was made of wood. This short weapon was carried across the front of the lower abdomen, hanging horizontally from the warrior's belt, inside a scabbard made of leather. The cutting edge faced upward, with the handle conveniently placed for the user's right hand. A small side-knife, with its own leather scabbard, could be attached to the front of the short sword's scabbard. The francisca, like the seax, first came into use among the eastern Germani, but later became the 'national' weapon of the Franks (whose name apparently gave birth to the term francisca). It was a light axe, mostly designed to be thrown from distance. The francisca had an arch-shaped head, which widened towards the cutting edge and terminated in a prominent point at both the upper and lower corners. The top of the head was S-shaped or convex, with the lower portion curving inward and forming an elbow with the short wooden haft. According to ancient sources, Germanic warriors threw their light axes with incredible accuracy and the francisca was thus particularly feared by their opponents. Axes of the francisca type were quite popular in Anglo-Saxon England during the early decades of the Germanic conquest, but they later became rarely used.

Bows were not very popular among Anglo-Saxon warriors, being used for hunting but only rarely seen on battlefields. Anglo-Saxon bows were made from yew, ash or elm; they had a draw force of 100lb and an effective range of 200 metres. From a technical point of view they were longbows, since they were created from a single piece of wood. This was either cut from the centre of a tree trunk or worked from a branch of suitable shape and size. The overall height of an Anglo-Saxon bow generally corresponded to that of its user. When not in use, a bow was almost straight; when strung, it was nearly D-shaped in cross-section. Arrow shafts were cut from thin shoots created by coppicing the appropriate trees, while bowstrings were made of linen thread looped and bound into a cord. Arrowheads could be of three different kinds: blade-shaped, spike-shaped and chisel-shaped. Spike-shaped heads were specifically designed for combat use, with the other two also employed for hunting. Each arrowhead was fixed with a tang to its shaft, which had feathers applied at the opposite end to the head and was 65–75cm long.

Bibliography

Anderson, E.B., *Cataphracts: Knights of the Ancient Eastern Empires* (Pen & Sword, 2016)
Baker, P., *Armies and Enemies of Imperial Rome* (Wargames Research Group, 1981)
Bishop, M.C. & Coulston, J.C., *Roman Military Equipment from the Punic Wars to the Fall of Rome* (Oxbow Books, 2006)
Blair, J., *Building Anglo-Saxon England* (Princeton University Press, 2018)
Breay, C. & Story, J., *Anglo-Saxon Kingdoms: Art, Word, War* (British Library Publishing, 2018)
Brzezinski, R. & Mielczarek, M., *The Sarmatians 600 BC–AD 450* (Osprey Publishing, 2002)
Campbell, J., *The Anglo-Saxons* (Penguin, 1991)
Connolly, P., *Greece and Rome at War* (Macdonald Phoebus Ltd, 1981)
Cowan, R. & O'Brogain, S., *Roman Legionary AD 284–337* (Osprey Publishing, 2014)
Crossley-Holland, K., *The Anglo-Saxon World. An Anthology* (Oxford University Press, 2009)
Elliot, P., *Legions in Crisis: Transformation of the Roman Soldier AD 192–284* (Fonthill Media, 2014)
Elton, H., *Warfare in Roman Europe AD 350–425* (Clarendon Press, 1998)
Esposito, G., *The Late Roman Army* (Winged Hussar Publishing, 2016)
Fleming, R., *Britain after Rome: The Fall and Rise, 400 to 1070* (Penguin, 2011)
Goldsworthy, A., *The Fall of the West: The Slow Death of the Roman Superpower* (Weidenfeld & Nicolson, 2009)
Harrison, M., *Anglo-Saxon Thegn 499–1066 AD* (Osprey Publishing, 1993)
Heath, I., *Armies of the Dark Ages 600–1066* (Wargames Research Group, 1980)
Higham, N.J. & Ryan, M.J., *The Anglo-Saxon World* (Yale University Press, 2015)
Kiley, K.F., *An illustrated Encyclopedia of the Uniforms of the Roman World* (Lorenz Books, 2012)
Macdowall, S. & Embleton, G., *Late Roman Infantryman AD 236–565* (Osprey Publishing, 1994)
Macdowall, S. & Hook C., *Late Roman Cavalryman AD 236–565* (Osprey Publishing, 1995)
Macdowall, S. & McBride, A., *Germanic Warrior AD 236–568* (Osprey Publishing, 1996)
Nicasie, M., *Twilight of Empire: The Roman Army from the Reign of Diocletian until the Battle of Adrianople* (Brill Academic Publishers, 1998)
Nicolle, D., *Arthur and the Anglo-Saxon Wars* (Osprey Publishing, 1984)
Nicolle, D. & McBride, A., *Romano-Byzantine Armies 4th–9th Centuries* (Osprey Publishing, 1992)
Syvanne, I., *Military History of Late Rome 284–361* (Pen & Sword, 2014)
Travis, J. & Travis, H., *Roman Body Armour* (Amberley, 2012)
Travis, J. & Travis, H., *Roman Helmets* (Amberley, 2015)
Travis, J. & Travis, H., *Roman Shields* (Amberley, 2014)
Warry, J., *Warfare in the Classical World* (Salamander Books, 1997)

The Re-enactors Who Contributed to This Book

Protectores Domini Nostri

The group Protectores Domini Nostri aims to bring to life the Personal Guard, Concilium Principis and Imperial Comitatus of a Roman emperor in the period from the end of the third century to the beginning of the fourth, with particular reference to the reign of Emperor Maxentius (AD 306–312). Through the study of literary sources, iconography and the interpretation of archaeological finds, the group attempts to reconstruct the military and ceremonial aspect of the restricted imperial entourage of this specific time frame. The Protectores, the name of the chosen soldiers who were selected from among the best elements of the army ranks to serve under the Augusti, were presumably all former officers and through their service at court were projected to embark on a career that would lead them to the highest posts. The name chosen for the group originates from a funerary inscription found in Rome, where a certain Valerius refers to himself in the inscription precisely as *PROTECTOR DOMINI NOSTRI MAXENTI AVGVSTI*. In addition to the Protectores, the group also reconstructed a Late Imperial legion, that of the Moesiaci Seniores, a unit attested at the time of Maxentius in the north-eastern Italian fortresses of Aquileia and Verona. The president of the group, Marco Cecini, has attempted to reconstruct the figures of Emperors Maxentius and Aurelian (AD 270–275), with a thorough investigation of the available iconographic and literary sources, especially numismatic ones, which are essential for a correct understanding of the imperial clothing of the period of interest. The group has collaborated with a local Italian television station, Canale 10, on the production of popular historical content, and is working on the completion of a self-produced documentary on the life of Emperor Maxentius.

Contacts:
Email: protectoresaugusti@gmail.com
Facebook: https://www.facebook.com/ProtectoresAugusti/

Letavia

Letavia is a living history/re-enactment group based in Brittany, focusing on the Late Antique and Early Medieval periods. The main focus of the group is on the fifth century AD in Brittany and the British Isles, extending into the ninth–tenth centuries AD (the period of the Kingdom of Brittany that resisted invasion by the Franks) and the eleventh century with the beginning of the feudal period.

Contacts:
Facebook: https://www.facebook.com/letavia.teulu

Wulfheodenas

Wulfheodenas is a living history society which seeks to recreate the military aristocracy, their warrior retinues and the mead hall culture of the sixth–seventh-century Northern world. Wulfheodenas is the Old English equivalent of the Old Norse *ulfheðna'r*, meaning 'wolf coats'. Our emblem is derived from a pressblech foil from Fen Drayton, Cambridgeshire. The foil depicts a weapon bearing a wolf-headed warrior and is one of a small number of similarly executed figures known from Northern Europe. We began operating nearly twenty years ago and were the first group that dedicated itself to the study and portrayal of the cultures of the late sixth and early seventh centuries. Members have always relied on serious research and excellent crafts skills.

Contacts:
Facebook: https://www.facebook.com/Wulfheodenas/?ref=page_internal

Uttaharjar

Uttaharjar is a history society founded in the Vendel Parish of Sweden in 2017, and consists of members from Sweden, Norway and Denmark. The focus of its activities is on the Scandinavian Vendel period (*c.* AD 500–800). This coincides with the Frankish Merovingian period (AD 500–751) and the English Early to Middle Anglo-Saxon period (AD 410–850). Members of the society recreate and inform about the Vendel period's artefacts from Sweden, Norway and Denmark. The primary focus is on the upper social strata of the Vendel society. Members of the society have researched and reconstructed grave finds from Lovö, Ultuna, Vendel, Valsgärde, Tuna in Badelunda, Broa on Gotland and Kobbeå on Bornholm, and continue to expand the research on Vendel archaeology. Clothes, household items, tools, weapons, helmets and various accessories are recreated and tested in a period-typical way in as close to period-typical environments as possible, with the goal of scientifically recreating the conditions for an experiential approach to Vendel history. The society collaborates with several museums and educational institutions such as universities and schools, as well as with other re-creation groups having similar purposes around Europe (in countries including England, Germany, France and Italy).

Contacts:
Facebook: https://www.facebook.com/share/12HQLgyN2AJ/?mibextid=wwXIfr

Index